FIGHTING FOR THE KING

By the same author

Catherine Booth
Bramwell Booth
Messages To Messengers

FIGHTING FOR THE KING

CATHERINE
BRAMWELL-BOOTH

HODDER AND STOUGHTON
LONDON SYDNEY AUCKLAND TORONTO

British Library Cataloguing in Publication Data

Booth, Catherine Bramwell
Fighting for the King.
1. Christian life
I. Title
248.4 BV4501.2

ISBN 0 340 33141 0

 Printed in Great Britain for Hodder and Stoughton Limited, Mill Road, Dunton Green, Sevenoaks, Kent by Cox & Wyman Limited, Reading, Berks. Photoset by Rowland Phototypesetting Limited Bury St Edmunds, Suffolk.

Hodder and Stoughton Editorial Office: 47 Bedford Square, London WC1B 3DP

'Catherine Bramwell-Booth's enchanting verses, published on her hundredth birthday, will delight and edify all Christians of whatever denomination. Her own sure faith over a long life shines out of them, and the artistry of her choice of words and simple rhythms makes them a joy, read or recited or sung. We made one another's acquaintance a long time ago, and now FIGHTING FOR THE KING will ensure her continuing presence. The King to be fought for is, of course, Jesus, and the troops Christian Soldiers of the Salvation Army, into which Commissioner Catherine was born.'

Malcolm Muggeridge

'If it needs the overflow of heart to give the lips full speech, then in these pages are to be found those living springs at which the thirsty spirit may freely drink and be richly refreshed. For this reason, albeit if only in this small way, I am glad to share in the celebrations of Commissioner Catherine's one hundredth birthday.'

General Frederick Coutts

To my youngest sisters, Olive and Dora,
who by their love make our home
a heaven below

Contents

Preface 3

Father, Son And Holy Spirit 9

Speaking To God 39

Salvation Army Warfare 69

The Beauty Of Creation 89

In Sorrow And In Joy 117

Experience 151

On Death And Eternity 199

Index of First Lines 213

Preface

My childhood was an interesting one – quite different from that of children today. I was educated by my mother. Speaking to a conference of Salvation Army social workers in 1921 on 'The Care and Training of Children', my mother said much that revealed the philosophy behind her own children's upbringing.

> God's plan for children is that their mother should be young with them. [My mother was not yet twenty-two when I was born.] Though human beings are so much alike, it is the differences that are vital. This is especially so with children; and this is why we cannot deal with children except individually . . . If you want a clever child, an original child, he or she must have plenty to do, plenty to make . . . Every child possesses a creative instinct in one direction or another: it is very important that this should be encouraged and developed . . . A child must not only have something to do, something to make: there must be someone to admire the finished work . . .

My verse, I think, is the outcome of such a philosophy, and I am grateful that my mother pursued that approach in bringing up her seven children.

This was not the only philosophy shaping my early life. The *Daily Telegraph* of 23 October 1883 described 'The Salvation Army Christening' – the occasion when General William Booth, my grandfather, dedicated me to God in the presence of my parents and a typically lively early-day Salvation Army congregation. He said:

It is the principle of The Salvation Army that everything we have or possess belongs to God; that the misery of the world commenced with rebellion against God and in believing that we could manage better for ourselves than God could manage for us. We hold it to be a principle of true godliness, true religion, that we should go back to God and give Him our hearts, our lives, and all we possess. This father and mother are here tonight carrying out that principle, and in the presence of this congregation and before all the holy angels, bring the dearest, choicest treasure with which God has entrusted them, and offer this dear, precious child up to Him, and engage that they will train, and nurture, and strengthen it to be not only a child but a servant of the living God, and a good Soldier of Jesus Christ, to fight His battles and take His lot . . .

Thus my life was set in the direction of fighting for the King of kings.

From then on, wherever my mother went on Salvation Army service, I went too, taking my naps in an empty clothes basket or a drawer, lying on a pillow my mother brought, depending on what local circumstances offered. So it was that at ten months I accompanied her to Paris where my Aunt Katie was in her third year of seeking to establish the Army amidst fierce opposition. Whilst we were there, a letter came from my father telling my mother that the Army's rescue work for girls was growing apace, and that she was needed to organise it. A few weeks later, therefore, with me in her arms, this young Salvationist was to be seen threading her way through the narrow streets of Whitechapel, shouted at by roughs, a target for cabbage stalks and other refuse. A well aimed potato caught her on the side of her head, but this was interpreted by her as a seal to her venture; 'God is going to make this work a blessing, and the Devil is stirred up in opposition,' she said to herself. And she was right on both counts. As for me, two days before my first birthday

I was introduced to the Army's newly begun social work for women – a work of which, in a much expanded form, I was to become leader more than forty years later. I thrived on my accompanying role, and my deep love for my mother is evident in several of my verses about her.

My earliest recollection of that other powerful influence upon my life, my father, was when I was about three years old. The picture my mind clearly sees, like a light patch in surrounding darkness, is myself holding my father's hand, to which mine reaches up, and we two walking down the passage into his office and across to the window. Here I am lifted up to peep into a nest of white mice. He talks to me about the 'dear little things', and I have loved mice ever since. As we grew older we kept all manner of pets and these were his special interest. What excitement when he brought home some new 'person' from the city! He advised on all matters concerning them, and we were occasionally allowed to 'sit up late' to show him fresh arrivals or to be comforted for some tragic loss. He inspired in each of us an intense devotion to dumb creatures. He could make us feel that even spiders and fleas had their good points!

Papa came down stairs with me once in the middle of the night because I had heard a strange sound from the 'animal' shed. We found the hedgehog had got out of his cage and was eating our favourite and oldest guinea-pig, queen of all the guinea-pigs! The queer part was that although she paused to make, for a guinea-pig, horribly loud cries, she then resumed the eating of a lettuce leaf! How tenderly my father cared for the little creature, comforted me and gave me instructions on how to nurse the invalid. She recovered.

To hear my father pray on those occasions when, not having gone to the office as early as usual, he took family prayers instead of our mother, made us realise that he knew God was near. God was a friend with Whom my father talked. He taught me to pray, and many of the verses in this collection are simply my talks with God.

Family prayers were no formality. We children were allowed to bring any instruments we could play; a drum and a triangle for the little ones. The custom introduced by our mother was to sing the same song for a week, so that we might learn the words; the verses were read out for the benefit of those who could not yet read. One of the younger ones sat on my father's knee, and he made remarks about the Bible portion as he read, which explained and applied it. Often he addressed his comments to the child on his knee, who sometimes commented too. Some of the verses in *Fighting for the King* are centred upon my father.

As the eldest of our family of five girls and two boys, I was the first to leave home to train as a Salvation Army officer. I was not yet twenty. My parents and aunts and uncles, as the first generation of Salvationists, had all begun work in some post of responsibility; each of *us*, however, at our father's desire and rather to the amusement of the General, our grandfather, came up through the ranks. My mother wrote at the time:

> It is a very deep and true joy . . . but the losing her from home cannot be other than very painful to us, and for my own part, I wonder how I can manage without her, and whether I shall not be compelled to relax in some measure my outside work. Catherine has now, for years, been a very real right hand in the home, and yet this step which she is taking is, after all, the flowering of all our hopes and desires for her . . .

Speaking at a public meeting in the Cannon Street Hotel some time later, I emphasised that I was a Salvation Army officer by conviction and choice, and not because my dear parents were Salvationists. I explained that I had considered the various agencies and organisations that existed for the saving of souls and benefiting the destitute, and in none had I seen so many opportunities for the doing of this work by women as were afforded in The

Salvation Army. What I declared with such conviction at twenty, I still maintain today. My verses about Salvation Army life are a result of that conviction. Apart from a brief period in corps (pastoral) work at the beginning, my forty-five years of active officership were divided between the training of officer-cadets, responsibility at various levels for the Army's work in Europe after two world wars, leadership of the women's social work, and literary work.

Amongst those I thank for their help I include my father who called trees his friends and taught me to gaze in wonder at the beautiful shape of trees, even when bare of leaves, and the glory of the Autumn and the delicate colours of Spring. As children our book world was largely peopled by our father. He advised, discussed, made loans and sometimes gifts. He always added the admonition 'no fiction'. We early imbibed from him the notion that luxury consisted of a book, plus time.

My mother shared with us an artist's view of creation. Think of the loveliness of the sky at sunset, of the primrose or the bluebell wood! All God's invention. I often find myself in communion with the Creator, thanking Him for inventing colour and giving me eyes to see it: a field of mustard in bloom; poppies, their scarlet glory suddenly flashed before our eyes; corn, golden in the evening light of Autumn. Sad, I think, that there are still so many who are blind to the beauties of our earthly dwelling. God created beauty for our joy, giving us eyes to recognise it. Paul says, 'Let your requests be made known unto God with thanksgiving.' I find myself constantly thanking the Creator for inventing such loveliness for us. Beauty is linked together with our vision by the poets, who express our feelings.

At one time 'Words that came by night' was considered as a subtitle to this little book. Now I find that this phrase exactly describes some of the contents. At night when I cannot sleep I often turn a thought into a line. As I lie awake a thought often possesses the mind in a rhythm that governs following lines. Sometimes a group of lines make a verse. They come as a message to my own heart or as fitting for one I love, never with any thought of publication. But when it was suggested that they might be of help to others if published, I was delighted and felt that it was almost too good to be true, when Messrs Hodder & Stoughton accepted them.

I thank God for the encouragement my two sisters, Olive and Dora, who share my home, have given me. We pray together that some heart may find a message in these pages and I thank God for sending me literary help by His child, my comrade in The Salvation Army, Major Jenty Fairbank.

Catherine Bramwell-Booth.

1983.

FATHER, SON AND HOLY SPIRIT

Psalm Of Praise

COME and praise the Lord with me
For His loving kindness;
All my sins He's pardoned me,
Healed my soul of blindness:
Now my eyes behold His beauty,
Christ is altogether lovely!

Come and praise the Lord with me,
I, so poor, so fearing;
He receives and comforts me
By His word endearing:
Changeless are His love and mercy,
Christ is altogether lovely!

Come and praise the Lord with me
For His keeping power,
Daily strength He's giving me,
Grace for every hour:
Now my soul is led on safely,
Christ is altogether lovely!

Come and praise the Lord with me
For the promise given
Of a place prepared for me
With Him in His Heaven:
Everlasting, tender, holy,
Christ is altogether lovely!

God With Us

And they heard the voice of the Lord God walking in the garden in the cool of the day. . . *Gen*. 3:8

Behold, I stand at the door, and knock: if any man hear my voice, and open the door, I will come in to him, and will sup with him, and he with me. *Rev*. 3:20

I

OH! Strange, that from the dim mysterious past
Of this our little world, hung midst the vast
Unmeasured universe, there should emerge,
All vivid and complete upon time's verge
This clear yet unimaginable sight –
God seeking man! Oh! Hateful guilty fright
That turned man's face away from Him and made
A gloomy hiding place of some fair glade
In that all-radiant garden God had planned
For man's delight; giv'n him, that human hand
Might share with the divine the living joy
Of making beauty; and employ
His powers, and in the musical cool eve
Wander with His Creator and receive
The story of creation, how it came,
Until his heart and mind are all aflame
With inspiration from the thoughts of God!
How has man fallen to become the clod
You see! Yet, deep within his breast, still is
A spark of that pure fire which once was his,
Before sin stifled its up-leaping light.
And still 'tis in a garden, in the sight

Of flowers, when evening quietly doth fall,
That man doth know a loneliness that all
His human loves and friendships cannot heal.
It is the creature calling for the seal
Of intercourse with his Creator; He
Alone can satisfy man's heart, and be
The Comforter of every soul He lends
To earth!
Oh! Strange, that man should make him friends
Of all that live, while he yet turns aside
From God Who still is seeking, far and wide
About the troubled earth, as once He sought
In Eden him whom sin to shame had brought.
Yea, as a careful shepherd who doth seek
His straying sheep in danger on the bleak
Inhospitable hills, so doth the Lord,
King of creation, seek lost souls. Adored
By seraphim and cherubim, He yet
Doth seek for man on whom His love is set.
Oh wonderful! Oh beautiful! Oh far
Beyond man's highest dreams of mercy are
God's ways! Who from the cradle of his race
Seeks man with everlasting love and grace.

II

What sight and sound is this of One Who stands
And beats upon a fast-closed door? His hands
Are wounded each, and in His eye there dwells
The eager look of listening love which tells
Of hope deferred but not despoiled; of haste
That can be patience too. There is that traced
Upon His brow that only sorrow leaves
Upon the head God loves. For he who grieves
With God the beautifying touch doth bear
Mere joy could never give; then He, Who there
Stands at that mean and silent threshold, must
Know more of grief than ever human dust
Alone could bear; yea, and He must be more

Close-kin to God; for no man ever bore
A countenance whereon so clearly shone
Pure loveliness; as though God had put on
A robe of flesh and made Him very man!
Ah! He so earnest knocking surely can
Be One alone of all who ever trod
The earth: Jesus, the living Son of God!
He is the Giver Who, when every gift
Is garnered in the house, the latch would lift
That His best gift of love might be
By His own presence ratified; shall He
Find that the door is barred against Him? Strange,
Men choose to shut out God! For in the range
Of merely human thought where could be found
A sequel so amazing as this sound,
This knocking, this astounding precious sight,
God standing suppliant at man's door, the light
From His fair form illuminating all
The darkness of man's heart and mind? No wall
Of separation now remains but this –
Man's will to be shut off from what is his,
To choose him other joys and other gods
Whose tyrannies but multiply the rods
Which vex his soul! Oh, slow is man to learn
What to his peace belongs! Oh, swift to turn
His trust to any new-fledged lie that chirps,
And thus, the father of all lies usurps
The throne prepared for truth in every heart;
Whilst Christ, Who is the truth, must wait apart.
He will not cross, almighty though He be,
The bound'ry within which man's will is free;
Unsought, Love cannot lift man from sin's mire;
Until man's will doth join with his desire!
Then shall the door be suddenly thrown wide
And Christ, Who knocked, shall enter and abide.

III

The house was swept and garnished, for the Lord
Had heard my cry for help and by His word
The enemy was driven forth. My sins
He had forgiv'n, one who anew begins
His life was I; resolved of this one thing:
That Jesus of my heart should be the King!
For has He not made all things new, restored
The glory of the day and freshly poured
Into night's cup the rest it had not held
For years? And now that evil was expelled
I dared to hope that, searching, I should find
Some path of willing service to mankind
That I might tread for Jesus' sake; for I,
Who love Him, know that love can thrive but by
A daily giving in His name. Thus passed
The busy, joyful days, until at last
I found me wearying, perplexed by woes
That burdened other hearts, and by old foes
Who presently approached my soul to seek
Some means of entry, luring me to speak.
Now, though my will was set to follow Christ,
Yet were there moments when a thought sufficed
To wake desire for some forbidden fruit,
Or for that company which would pollute;
Thus though my good desires did not abate,
Nor my endeavour for the right, my state
Was restless. Then the evening silence brought
A footfall to my listening ear. I thought
I heard the well-loved voice. Hope leaped in me
And straightway up crept fear, for how could He
I hoped for tarry here? Had I but more – !
And mazed 'twixt hope and fear, Love to the door
Did draw me and I heard Him say, 'I will
Come in and sup with thee.' Then did joy fill
My heart, my door I opened, and the Lord
All beautiful in love sat at my board!
Yea, at my frugal board did break my bread.

With His own blessèd hands, bowed His dear head
In prayer for me! How grew my chamber light!
How hallowed every stick that in His sight
Took on new grace! Christ's glory did illume
My little all. Thus did my life assume
New dignity, for that I shared it all
With Him: new worth, for that, however small
My task, it is to Him I offer it
Who still doth dwell with me on whom is writ
His likeness, growing every day more clear.
For when Christ is so intimately near
All other gain and loss to man grows dim,
The beauty of the Lord begins to rest on him.
This is a secret none may know but he
With whom the Lord doth sup. That one shall see
The glory of his God in Christ, and prove
Each day in Christ, the Father's perfect love!

Christ's Return

. . . Christ Jesus came . . . to save sinners . . .
1 *Tim*. 1:15

. . . He cometh . . . every eye shall see Him . . .
Rev. 1:7

LOOK to the past's long night,
See dayspring's dawning light,
Christ promised!

To Bethlehem's stable cave,
A Saviour strong to save
He came!

Look through the future's gate
And work and watch and wait.
He cometh!

Love's Revealing

. . . God in the face of Jesus Christ.
II *Cor*. 4:6

. . . while we were yet sinners, Christ died . . .
Rom. 5:8

THAT men might see God, Jesus clothed
  Himself in clay;
Came down to earth and gave us Christmas day;
And lest His shining bind the soul
Beyond the will's control,
All kingly glory shed,
Laid low His lordly head
In weakness, took His rest
Upon His mother's breast;
That *I* might see Him and be unafraid,
The King of kings was in a manger laid.

That men might hear God, Jesus lived and spoke
  as man;
Sorrowed and joyed as but a brother can;
And lest His might should blind the mind,
He gentle, meek and kind
To manhood grew, then stood
Revealed unsullied Good.
Eternal Love drew thus
A listening ear from us.
That *I* might hear Him, yet be free to choose,
God's Truth appeared as Word I might refuse!

That we might know God, Jesus died to prove
Him Love,
Reaching our depths to lift our souls above;
And lest His holiness but told
How strong our guilt to hold,
Loved, while we sinners were,
Became for all who err
New living Way for men
To find their God again.
That *I* might know God and yet not despair,
My Saviour died, His life with me to share!

When Christ Was Born In Bethlehem

. . . Jesus was born in Bethlehem . . .
Matt. 2:1

. . . a Saviour, which is Christ the Lord.
Luke 2:11

[Jesus said] . . . I am the light of the world.
John 9:5

WHEN Jesus came to Bethlehem
To guide men,
To be a star and sun for them,
New light came down for me there,
New light for sinners everywhere,
When Jesus came to Bethlehem.

When Christ was born in Bethlehem
To save men,
To live and die and rise for them,
New hope was born for me there,
New hope for sinners everywhere,
When Christ was born in Bethlehem.

When God appeared in Bethlehem
To love men,
To save and keep and comfort them,
New peace was found for me there,
New peace for sinners everywhere.
New light, new new hope, new peace for thee,
New light, new hope, new peace for me
For alway,
For this day and every day,
Since God appeared in Bethlehem!

My God

. . . Emmanuel . . . God with us.
Matt. 1:23

. . . Christ . . . leaving us an example.
1 *Pet.* 2:21

HE speaks in language I can understand,
His hand can reach down low to take my hand;
His eye sees far ahead and guides my feet,
Whether through desert or by waters sweet;
His arm is strong enough to bear me up,
He bids my weary soul have rest and sup;
His heart is large enough to take me in,
And for His love of me, forgive my sin.
My God is more than all that I can tell,
Holy, Eternal, yet Emmanuel!
And His will is that I, poor wayward clod,
Should in simplicity be like my God!

All In Christ

But we see Jesus . . .
Heb. 2:9

Jesus saith . . . I am the way, the truth and the life. . .
John 14:6

THOU art the Way!
Can my rebellious feet
Find them a way more sweet?
Or wandering wide
From early morn to eventide,
Trace out a way more straight
From gate of hell to Heaven's gate?
From fleshly clod
To heart of God?

Thou art the Truth!
Can my unresting mind
By constant searching find
To 'Why?' and 'How?'
Answer more perfect than art Thou?
Solving life's silent riddle
As when the bow to fiddle
The master's touch unites
And in the doing smites
From those dumb entities
A wealth of harmonies.
Thus, being what Thou art,
Gives meaning to my heart,
Makes of my separate soul
Part of Thy music's whole,
Of ordered death
Immortal breath!

Thou art the Life!
Can hungry heart be fed
By any other bread?
Be satisfied
Except by knowing Thee? Who died
And passed through death to prove
God's everlasting Love
The source, support and goal
Of man's immortal soul.
Thus knowing Thee, man sees,
Whether in stars or trees,
Love's language writ;
God's thoughts by beauty lit
And the vast universe
Life's garment; time, man's nurse.

Believing thus, man lives, strives hopes and sings,
Prepares his soul for wings;
Knowing that Thou art life, he knows
Solace in all his woes,
Trusts Thy love's ruling good,
Thy Word, his spirit's food.
Thy triumph, man's free choice
To follow Thee and own Love's voice;
Leave dark for light and trust
In Thee, not that he must,
But that he knows of none
Save Jesus Christ, God's Son,
Who answers every need,
Who is man's Lord indeed,
Jesus, Who died, yet lives to be my Saviour.

Lord, join my little day
To Thine Eternity,
Quicken abundantly
Thy life in me,
Thy love in me be
Life and Truth and Way
Alway.

Lower Than Angels

But we see Jesus, Who was made a little lower than the angels. . .

Heb. 2:9

LOWER than angels Jesus came,
Wearing for us His human frame,
Bearing for us our meed of shame,
Thus Jesus came.

Lovingly, gently, Jesus spoke
Tenderly to the heart that broke,
Mightily so the dead awoke,
Thus Jesus spoke.

Lone in the mountain Jesus prayed;
Weeping, by Lazarus' grave new-made;
With agony, in garden shade,
Thus Jesus prayed.

High on a cross Christ Jesus died,
Praying for those who pierced His side,
Drawing men to Him from far and wide,
Thus Jesus died.

Quietly, early, Jesus rose;
Smiling, from grave to garden goes,
First Himself to a woman shows,
Thus Jesus rose.

Up into Heaven Jesus went,
Leaving a group of men intent
Spreading the Gospel He had sent,
Thus Jesus went.

Yet by His Spirit Jesus stays,
Companions all who walk His ways,
Shares with them each their strife of days,
Thus Jesus stays!

Low They Laid Him

. . . and laid Him in a manger; because there was no room for them in the inn.

Luke 2:7

And with Him they crucify two thieves. . .

Mark 15:27

OH, low they laid Him at His birth!
A manger for His natal bed,
The lowing beasts about His head;
The earthen floor, a heap of hay,
His mother's only bed that day.
Beyond the open door the scent
Of fields and flowers came and went;
And when the dawn had lit the sky
The village men went trooping by
To work; and some did stay and peep
At Mary's new-born Babe asleep;
For shepherds had been heard to say
A star had shown them where He lay
Who, born a prince, should bring men peace.
But many smiled and said, 'Is this
A fitting place for kingly seed?
He who lies here lies low indeed!'
Oh, low they laid Him at His birth!

Oh, low they laid Him at His death!
A thorn-crown for His kingly head,
A ribald soldiery to shed
His royal blood, justice defied,
It was a felon's death He died;
Cast out, derided and forgot,
While for His garment they cast lot;
And His dear body lifted up
That men might see Him drain the cup
Of bitterness, draw His last breath,
His ardent spirit stilled in death.
But some who went to see that sight
Smote on their breasts and cried, 'No night
Can be so dark as is this day,
When Jesus in a grave they lay;
Jesus, Who came to bless and save,
Who loved the sinners He forgave.
Jesus, Who made our hearts to sing,
Jesus, Who should have been our King.'
Oh, low they laid Him at His death!

Oh, low they laid Him at His birth,
Who came to bless the suffering earth,
And give her children rest from sin
That they and theirs might enter in
To life and Heaven with Him! And He,
Shall He be set aside by me?

Oh, low they laid Him at His death,
Who lives for evermore, and saith,
'I am the Bread of Life, the Way,
The Truth; let all men hear Me say,
"Come unto Me and live!"' And He,
Shall He be set aside by me?

Not To Destroy

For the Son of man is not come to destroy men's lives, but to save them. . . *Luke* 9:56

NOT to destroy, but to save,
Not to destroy but to build,
Not to destroy but to give us life,
This hath the Father willed.

Not to destroy but to seek,
Not to destroy but to find,
Not to destroy but to pardon all,
This is Christ Jesu's mind.

Not to destroy but to teach,
Not to destroy but bring light,
Not to destroy but to fill with joy,
This is the Spirit's might.

Father and Son, Holy Ghost,
Leading in truth to our Home,
Not to destroy but to save and keep,
Glorious the Son is come!

All As Thou Wilt

TO Christ thy King
O poor heart come
And worshipping,
Bow low and pray
And say:
All as Thou wilt,
Who knoweth how to bless;
All as Thou wilt,
Who faileth not in tenderness;
All as Thou wilt,
Whose wisdom is complete;
All as Thou wilt,
Whose love can make the bitter sweet;
My Lord, my Life, my Love,
All as Thou wilt.

Thy Rod

'. . . whom the Lord loveth He chasteneth. . .'
Heb. 12:6

COME with Thy rod, O Lord, and make my
languid zeal
The smart of love's sharp chastisement to feel.
Yea, with Thy rod! Lest I the deeper anguish know,
The pain of a forsaken sinner's woe.

Come with Thy rod, O Lord, make sleeping
conscience start,
That it may prick and trouble my dull heart.
Better Thy rod than that my soul should learn
to be
At peace with sin, at enmity with Thee.

Come with Thy rod, O Lord, smite my untutored
mind
That tears may give it sight the truth to find.
Spare not Thy rod! Cause me to bear its present
smart,
That I may be a child after Thy heart.

Blessed be Thy rod, O Lord! Its healing stripes
do give
Sure token that Thy love for me doth live:
Blessed be Thy rod! Its wounds do bring forth
strength to win
Uncompromising victory over sin.

A Selfish Prayer

'. . . let your requests be made known unto God.'
Phil. 4:6

OH, let there be
Enough for me
Of love,
To keep me from the coldness
Of this world and its oldness!

Oh, let there be
Enough for me
Of faith,
To keep my mind from yielding
To theories men are wielding!

Oh, let there be
Enough for me
Of light,
To keep my feet from falling
In sin when it is calling!

Oh, let there be
Enough for me
Of hope,
To keep my song inspired
When all my flesh is tired!

Oh, let there be
Enough for me
Of fear,
To keep alive the fire
Of all holy desire!

Oh, let there be
Enough for me
Of joy,
To keep my work a pleasure
That I give without measure!

Oh, let there be
Enough for me
Of rest,
To keep me from the hurry
Of overstrain and worry!
Of rest,
Oh, let there be
Enough for me!

A Prayer In The Land Of The Fells

THE hills are clothed with majesty,
The little hills with beauty;
Wrapped round by Heaven's immensity
They lift their heads in surety.

The streams flow down unceasingly,
And as they flow, sing sweetly;
They find their bourne unerringly,
And finding, meet it fitly.

Canst Thou not give me steadfastness,
Who gave the hills their fastness?
As streams find bourne, let blessedness
Be found by my heart's blindness!

Oh! still my mind's wild questioning,
And teach my heart the meaning
Of faith that lives by triumphing
And love that gives by giving.

If My Heart Should Falter

IF my heart should falter in a time of stress,
Jesus, stoop to me!
Speak to me in pity, touch in tenderness,
I would cleave to Thee!
All my mind's intention toward Thy will is set,
All my heart's desire is to trust Thee, yet,
Lest my will should waver, lest my faith should fail,
Shield me by Thy mercy, let not hell prevail.

If my heart should harden to a call of need,
Jesus, stoop to me!
Look on me with sadness, show me hands that
  bleed,
I would be like Thee!
I would show Thy pity, Thy dear charity,
I would cry forgiveness to mine enemy,
But lest wounds and sorrow turn my heart to stone,
Melt it by Thy love, Lord; save by love alone.

Mystery

'. . . I am not come to call the righteous, but sinners to repentance.' *Matt.* 9:13

O CHRIST! Would I had ever been all clean!
Yet 'tis my sin
Will let me in
To Heaven and Thee!
For were I righteous all
I'd hear no call
To run, to crawl
In rue to Thee.

Let There Be

'. . . they took knowledge of them, that they had been with Jesus.' *Acts* 4:13

JESUS, oh let there be on me,
For any other soul to read,
The marks of Thy dear company,
That all may know in very deed
I walk with Thee!

O Jesus, let there be in me,
For any other soul to share,
Thy love, the love of Calvary,
That I may show men everywhere
Thou liv'st in me!

Prevent Me, Lord

PREVENT me, Lord, from going where I would,
If there I may not company with Thee;
If on the way I choose to go there be
No brother's heart in need, to whom I could
Bring some of love and hope. And if I should
Forget this prayer and, striving to be free
From Thy restraining hand, attempt to flee,
Then wilt Thou hold me, bind me for my good.
For though the way I sought was very fair,
How, lacking Thee, should I discern its grace?
How taste its pleasures, if I could not share
Their sweets with Thee? Teach me, O Lord, that
in the place
To which desire has been the *only* guide,
Desire will ever be unsatisfied.

Morning Prayer

'. . . Jesus Himself drew near, and went with them.'
Luke 24:15

COME, blessed Jesus, come;
Draw near and walk with me,
That through each day in all I do
I may be led by Thee.
The little that I have,
O Lord, is all Thine own,
My burning heart with Thee would walk
And never walk alone.

Come, blessed Jesus, come;
Draw near and speak with me,
That I afresh may understand
The things concerning Thee:
Thy mind to me impart,
Let me Thy law receive,
Thy law of faith, Thy law of love,
Thy word believe and live.

Come, blessed Jesus, come;
Break bread again for me;
Lord open Thou my eyes that I
Thy living self may see.
Then joy shall fill my heart,
My strength be all renewed
To witness of Thy death and life,
By Thine own power endued.

Written to be sung to the tune Diademata.

Look On My Heart, Lord

LOOK on my heart Lord, read the word unspoken,
Story of sorrow, failure and of shame;
Now, by Thy word let all sin's power be broken,
Take Thou my heart and seal it with Thy Name;
Purge out its dross and sanctify its treasure,
Take it, keep it, ever Thine own.

Refrain:
Jesus! Jesus! Take the heart I yield Thee,
Take it and keep it ever Thine alone;
Purge out its dross and sanctify its treasure,
Take it, keep it, ever Thine own.

Speak to my heart, Thy word of love and power,
Give me again the peace of sins forgiven;
Faith trembling claims Thy help this very hour,
Now from my heart let every doubt be driven;
Cleanse and restore, make fit for Thine indwelling,
Take it, keep it, ever Thine own.

Take my poor heart Lord, guide and guard and
  fashion,
Mark on my mind the image of Thy love;
Kindle in me the flame of Thy compassion,
Show me Thy face, and fix my hopes above;
Here is my heart, to trust, serve and adore Thee,
Take it, keep it, ever Thine own.

Written for a tune that came into my head.

Thine, Lord, The Whole

LORD let Thy tenderness
Stoop down to me,
Gather my helplessness
Up unto Thee;
I am undone and cry,
Lord! Save me or I die,
Jesus I now on Thy love rely,
Come, set me free.

All that my shame would hide,
Sins I allow,
Selfishness, doubt and pride,
Confessing now;
I would be clean indeed,
From all base bondage freed;
Who can meet my longing heart's deep need,
Who Lord but Thou?

Come now, O Saviour King,
Possess my soul,
I yield up everything
To Thy control;
Come, here and now, and take
My guilty heart and make
There a temple hallowed for Thy sake,
Thine Lord the whole.

Written to be sung to the tune Santa Lucia.

Work In Me

'. . . the Holy Ghost . . . He shall teach you. . .'
John 14:26

HOLY Spirit, work in me
All Thy will, that I may be
Throughly purged from every sin,
Sealed without and cleansed within.

Holy Spirit, take from me
All mine that could hinder Thee
Using me, to show Thy mind,
Just and merciful and kind.

Holy Spirit, give to me
All I need to follow Thee;
Eyes to see the sinner's need,
Heart to succour him indeed.

Holy Spirit, show to me
All through Thee I still may be;
Set my heart on things above,
On the sinner set my love.

For Friend What Shall I Pray?

'. . . ask what ye will. . .'
John 15:7

FOR friend what shall I pray?
What say
When kneeling at God's feet,
Repeat
What plea with strong desire,
Require
Straight to the ear of God
What good?
For God hath said to me
And thee
He'll be enquired of
In love,
Grant humble faith's request,
Make blest
The suppliant by His Spirit's
Merits.
For Christ will intercede,
Will plead,
So none comes to God's throne
Alone;
And poorest heart may dare
In prayer
Ask what it will and know,
Although
The asking be amiss,
Yet this
Prevents not God's reply.

And I,
When praying for another,
My brother,
Am granted glimpse free given
Of Heaven;
See there, by faith, Love reigning,
Love deigning
To over-rule earth's ill
And fill
(Past fear's reach to molest)
With rest
Each weary soul; so thine
And mine?

Then may my praying tend,
All end
On this key-note for ever
And ever
God work His lovely will,
Fulfil
His perfect thoughts for us,
And thus
Attuned I'll speak my best
Behest,
Ask this and that for thee,
So be
All's subject to this chief
Belief:
God's will is highest good,
Pure food
For all our hunger; I
Deny
All hopes, joys, plans, outside;
Confide
My every wish, above
To Love,
Who can transform and change,
Arrange

And make my praying match,
As latch
To door, His purposes,
And bless
Asker and asked for, each,
And teach
The mind how to discern,
To learn,
How God's wise love will choose
And use
Our need, to fit His gift,
And lift
Our thirsting to drink up
God's cup.
Oh! then in all I pray,
Alway
I'll cry, first, last and through:
God do
His will on earth, in thee,
In me,
Then though my best wish
Perish,
Still cries my heart 'Amen!
Amen!'

Lord Let Me!

LORD! Let me walk
In Thy dear company;
For I would talk
With Thee.
Hear with a listening ear,
Through all life's changing way
All Thou wouldst say
To me.

Lord, let me work
The works Thou shalt appoint;
I will not shirk,
But be
Thy willing servant true,
Serving for love alone,
Love of a son
To Thee.

Lord Of My Life

NOT as mighty river
Bound in narrow bed,
But as winging bird
By instinct led:
Thus would I be
Drawn unto Thee
Lord of my life for ever.

Not as crystal flower
Dead before begun,
But as bud up-pressing
Drinks in the sun:
Thus would I be
Heart fixed on Thee
Lord of my life for ever.

Not as slave to master
Ever yielding lives,
But as love enraptured
To lover gives:
Thus would I be
Servant to Thee
Lord of my life for ever.

Do This In Me

O LORD of life Whose Name is Love,
Kindle Thy flame
In my poor heart,
Breathe on it there
That I may share
In what Thou art
And show Thy Name
To those who dwell with sin and death.
Burn with Thy fires
Selfish desires,
To zeal refine my weak endeavour,
O Lord of life
Do this in me,
And let Thy work endure forever.

O Lord Give Time

O LORD, give time for earthly knowing,
Here, where the soul must pace
The limits of a spirit growing
To measure Thou dost trace.

Here, where the sun declines at noon,
Where moon departs for days,
Where all the flowers fade too soon
And men have ugly ways.

Lord, give my wonder-hungry heart
The time to peer and ponder,
To learn the joy of knowing part,
The bliss of growing fonder.

O Lord, give time for earthly knowing
Here let me learn to wait
The harvest that may follow sowing,
The gains that come too late!

Lord, Let Me In

[Jesus said] . . . where I am, there ye may be also.
John 14:3

Not by works of righteousness which we have done, but according to His mercy He saved us. . . *Titus* 3:5

LORD, let me in to where Thou art at last;
At last, Lord, let me in:
Not that I have a worthiness to be
Let in to Thee,
Nor that I bring
Treasure for Thy liking,
A gift to let me in,
Albeit the hands that offer are unclean. . .

If I had great possessions might it be
Thine eye would light on them and not on me?
And I slip in to Thee?
Ah, if I had, I'd try, not turn me sorrowful away
But eager offer all. . . ALL!
To be let in. . .

To be let in at last to where Thou art,
O Jesus, let it be!
Not that in me
Is any good to be approved by Thee,
Not even constancy
In turning from my sins, my doubts, my fears:
How often have I looked away from Thee
To that dark swirling sea,
The circumstances of my life piled high
By winds of men's or devil's ill intent,
And sinking then. . . Thy hand has saved me.
Jesus! Think but on this, Thy mercy!
Then, for Thy mercy's sake, hear my lament,
And in Thy mercy let me in to Thee.

Not that I have a right to be let in,
Oh no! This poor heart has no rights in Thee,
No claim, no deeds as plea,
Yet do I cry to Thee,
Christ Jesus, hear Thou me.
Lord, let me in to where Thou art at last,
Though every hope of betterment be past,
Though all the little things I thought I'd done,
Though all the conflicts that I thought I'd won
Are seen to be
But of Thine everlasting love to me
And any good in me not mine
But Thine. . .

Thine was the beauty taught me how to hate
My mean and narrow-margined selfish state,
Thy Word the light transfused my dark,
Showed me my sin,
Yet said, 'Forgiv'n!'
How could *that* be, but that Thy love was set
  on me?
Not that I loved Thee Lord, though
Thou knowest all things and Thou know'st I do,
But that Thou first lovest me,

And shed Thy blood for purging of my sin.
Lord, by Thy loving, by Thy dying, let me in;
That where Thou art, there I may also be with
Thee.

Jesus my Lord remember me,
Look on me from Thy throne
When I at last go down through death alone,
Remember me,
And let me in to where Thou art:
At last, Lord
Let me in.

The Kindness And Love Of God Our Saviour

O Love of God most precious,
O Love of God brought near,
O Love of God so tender-sweet
Weakest sinner need not fear.

O Love of God give pardon,
Myself I bring to be
A servant who is Thine alone,
Loving all for love of Thee.

O Love of God possess me
In each new day afresh,
So men may see what Thou art like
Showing through my veil of flesh.

O Love of God I trust Thee,
I rest in what Thou art,
When grief and darkness hide my path
Still Thou rulest in my heart.

Today! A Prayer On A Birthday

LET us together thank God for today!
Thank Him for today and say:
'Praise be to God we live today,
Today we live.' And giving thanks we say,
'Lord, grant us yet another day!'
For this we pray, and say,
Although we know it may
Bring sorrow,
'Please, dear Lord God,
Let us together see tomorrow.'

Day By Day

'. . . the government shall be . . . His . . .'
Isa. 9:6

KING Thou art of my heart:
Thine the governing
And the ordering
Of my way
Day by day.

Slave I am of the Lamb:
Mine the following
And in everything
I obey
Day by day.

Thanksgiving

THANK Thee, O Lord, for coming here
To show what God is like to me,
That I may worship without fear
The Holy One of Calvary.

Oh, thank Thee, Lord, for coming down
To tell me what I ought to be,
To please Him Who now wears the crown,
The holy crown of Calvary.

I thank Thee, Lord, for keeping all
Thy precious promises to me.
Now help me to obey the call
That comes to me from Calvary.

May I be by Thy spirit led
According to Thy word to me,
And daily by Thy presence fed
With power that flows from Calvary.

Happy I Could Be

'. . . Am I my brother's keeper?' *Gen.* 4:9

O LORD, how happy I could be
Here in the woods with Thee!
Marking Thy style in making trees,
Watching the flight of honey bees,
Or, lying by a bank of bracken,
Observe the fronds held taut, then slacken
As shadow-making wind goes by
Luring white clouds across the sky.
Oh, happy I could be
Alone with Thee,
Hadst Thou not made me lover,
Given me a brother!

O Lord, how happy I could be
Here in the fields with Thee!
Helping Thee sow the living seed,
Sharing in Thy creative deed,
Busy with hope-filled joyful pride
Of sweet dominion, at Thy side;
And meditating in the evening,
Peer at Thy plans, search out their meaning,
Piercing the lovely outer rind
Of Thy all perfect works to find
Thy thought that made them; and to fit
(Thy love illuminating it)
My need, to what I see Thou art,
Learn I am carried in Thy heart!

Oh, happy I could be
Alone communing in the fields with Thee,
Hadst Thou not made me lover,
Given me a brother,
Bid me his keeper be,
Hold him in trust for Thee.

A Lover's Sigh

O LORD! How great a joy had I some gift
Of value rare and manifest to place
Upon the altar of my love; some grace
That I might dedicate to Thee and lift,
From being earth's, to Heav'n; make thus a rift
In the dull grey of my endeavour, and trace
What once was mine to where, before Thy face,
It tells my love, clearer than words, more swift.
But if such joy be not for my delight
And I content with poverty must be,
Still, for my comfort, through the day and night,
Love shall stand ready, that Thou mayest see
With what glad preparation for its flight,
Love would yield up its best of gifts to Thee.

SALVATION ARMY WARFARE

An Army With Banners

Canticles 6:4

OH, have you seen the Army come marching
  down our street,
With timbrels, bands, and banners, and sound of
  tramping feet?
Their flags fly out,
They clap and shout,
And in and out
And all about
The music rolls a'thundering,
It sets my heart a'wondering.
Oh, have you seen the Army come marching
  down our street,
With timbrels, bands, and banners, and sound of
  tramping feet?

Oh, have you seen the Army come marching
  down our street?
The children rush to meet it, and oh, what dancing
  feet!
Some may be bare,
But who's to care?
The Army's there,
And all may share,
So round the march the children throng
And dance and leap the whole way long.
Oh, have you seen the Army come marching down
  our street?
The children rush to meet it, and oh what dancing
  feet!

Oh, have you seen the Army come marching down
our street,
A hundred children leaping before its coming feet?
And as they go
The flag sweeps low,
It seems as though
'Twould gather so
The dancing shouting crowd of them
And march away with all of them!
Oh, have you seen the Army come marching down
our street,
A hundred children leaping before its coming feet?

Oh, have you seen the Army come marching down
our street,
Sunshine on their instruments, the dust about their
feet?
They often stay
To sing and pray
And have their say
Then march away;
The people fall to pondering
The sin in which they're wandering.
Oh, have you seen the Army come marching down
our street,
Sunshine on their instruments, the dust about their
feet?

Oh, have you seen the Army come marching down
our street,
When wind and rain are beating upon their
mud-stained feet?
They speak of light,
Of Heaven bright,
Of strength to fight
For God and right;
And someone's sure to hear them say
That sinners can be saved today!

Oh, have you seen the Army come marching down
our street,
When wind and rain are beating upon their
mud-stained feet?

Oh! Why not join the Army, go marching down
the street,
And let Salvation tidings be carried by your feet
To those who wait
In sin and hate,
And lead them straight
For Heaven's gate?
For in the streets of every land
They wait the Army's helping hand!
Oh! Why not join the Army, go marching down
the street,
And let Salvation tidings be carried by your feet?

Based on my experience as Captain of The Salvation Army Walthamstow I Corps. Bogey was our colour sergeant.

Fight For Jesus

OH! Ev'ry land is filled with sin,
But trusting Jesus we shall win,
So fight away, fight away!

The devil's slaves in chains we see,
But Jesu's grace will set them free,
So fight away, fight away!

Chorus
We mean to fight for Jesus, we will, we will!
In every land we'll take our stand
To live and die for Jesus! We will, we will,
We'll live and die for Jesus.

An Old Sister Of Ours

HUNGER and the cold
And she is old;
Alone and old and cold!

Darkness and the street,
No safe retreat;
For her worn feet a street!

Silence and the night,
For her no light;
No hope in sight, and night!

Think you someone's care
Can find her there
With love to spare for care?

About Some Of The Lord's Children At Our Corps

. . . the Son of man is come to save that which was lost . . . and seeketh that which is gone astray. *Matt*. 18:11, 12

I

LITTLE Jinks was up to larks
Always losing his good marks!
And he often got turned out
For the way he played about
In the meetings. For the boys
Made the most appalling noise
When Jinks overturned the seat,
Set them all to stamp their feet.
Sister Sillikins said she
would give up her Company
If that boy were still allowed
To unsettle the whole crowd.
Very shortly after that
Jinks appeared in a felt hat,
Said he was too big to go
With the kids. Besides 'twas slow!
But he hung about the band
Said their playing was just grand!
Left off school and went to work,
Learned to idle and to shirk;
Took to smoking cigarettes,
Spitting, swearing, making bets;
Then he ran away one day,
Went to sea and sailed away.
Many said 'What a relief!
He's no good, that's my belief.'

But the Lord went out to seek him in the wild,
For He wanted little Jinks to be His child.

II

Phyllis Gay was very young,
And she liked to be among
Sporty chums about the town,
Walked the High Street up and down.
In the meeting, at the back,
She would sit, and look quite black
When the Y. P. Sergeant-Major
Spoke to her. She said, 'You wager
I'm not getting saved just yet,
Mean to have my fling, you bet!'
Up she got and out she pranced;
After that she went and danced
Every evening at a club,
Someone saw her in a pub!
Then she went off to the city,
Goody Jones said, 'More's the pity!'

But the Lord went out to seek her in the wild,
For He wanted Phyllis Gay to be His child.

III

Charlie Sniff was rather proud,
Played his cornet very loud;
He would never testify,
Some thought smoked upon the sly.
Treasurer said he doubted whether
Charlie Sniff had really ever
Been converted. Still he played
Solo cornet, and he stayed
To the meeting every night
If the band turned out all right;
But he never stayed to pray
After eight p.m. on Sunday;
He slipped out, put on a cap,
Went to walk with Millie Flapp!

Once the Captain said he thought
That the Census Locals ought
Plainly to inform the lad
That, unless he changed, he had
Better leave; but then they said,
'Who is to be found instead
Who can play one half so well?
After all one cannot tell
Whether he might not some day
Pray as well as he can play?'
Six months later Sniff resigned,
Joined the Town Band; left behind
Every scrap of faith and prayer,
Plunged into the world and there

The Lord went out to seek him in the wild,
For He wanted Charlie Sniff to be His child.

IV

Thomas Trench drank like a fish
And he only had one wish,
That today he might drink more
Than on any day before.
An unpleasant sight to meet,
He comes reeling down the street;
And the gentry on the Bench
Are quite sick of Thomas Trench.
Fourteen days' imprisonment
Fails to change his temperament!
But what is the Bench to do?
There's a puzzle set for you!
Even at the Army Corps
Some despise him more and more,
Say he is too dirty far
To come where decent people are!
When he listens to the band,
Young White wishes he'd not stand
Quite so close! And when the march
Sweeps toward the railway arch,

He will push his way in front
And the Captain gets the brunt
Of his railing, drunken wit,
Which is certainly not fit
For the children's listening ears.
Oh, he'd be a sight for tears
Had we not grown deaf and blind.
And it's really hard to find
Any good in this low creature
Who has spoiled his better nature,
Travelling ever farther in
To the wilderness of sin.

But the Lord goes out to seek him in the wild,
For He wants old Thomas Trench to be His child.

V

Listen! You who know your Lord.
Listen! You who have His word.
Have you never heard Him say,
'Come with Me, I lead the way,
Follow Me, into the wild,
Help Me find my wayward child'?
Think! Your word to little Jinks
Might be just one of the links
Joining his abysmal need
To God's power to save; and lead
Jinks back Home again, and then,
Help him rescue other men.
Gays and Sniffs are all around
Near enough to holy ground
To be helped for Christ to stand
If *you* offered them a hand.
Even old Tom Trench might be
Found one day and helped to see
Beauty in the King of kings,
And find healing in His wings.

Listen, you who *love* your Lord!
Listen, you who *trust* His word!
Christ the Lord is calling now from out the wild,
Will you follow Him, help Him find His wayward
child?

Seeking The Lost

We are seekers with Him of the lost.
W. Bramwell Booth

HOW blest it were to seek the lost with Thee!
To walk with Thee along the stony track
That leads into the wilderness where stray
The lost Thou cam'st to seek! But how attain
To such a piercing happiness? And how
Confess a longing so beyond the range
Of human hope or possibility?
Shall one so poor, so puny, dare aspire
To company with Thee, the Son of God?

Nay, but I dare; for Thou, dear Christ, didst turn
And look on me, who straight forgot my lack
And only saw Thy need, and heard Thee say,
'Come, follow Me, for where I am there shall
My servant be, seeking the lost with Me!'

At One

AT one with my Lord!
Or living or dying,
In sweetest accord
I'm walking and working with Jesus my Lord.

At one with my Lord!
In gladness or sadness,
Sustained by His word
I'm waiting and watching for Jesus my Lord.

At one with my Lord!
In teaching and preaching
I'm wielding his sword,
To win souls from Satan to Jesus my Lord.

Written to be sung to the tune Ardwick.

The Only Time Is Now

. . . Willing in the day of Thy power. . .
Ps. 110:3

WHEN the heart is ready,
Power wings the word!
When the heart is ready,
Two-edged and sharp the sword;
When the heart is ready,
The sinner knows his Lord!

How shall the heart make ready,
Hedged in by fear and doubt?
How shall the heart make ready,
With devils all about?
How shall the heart make ready?
By sending God a shout!

When shall the heart make ready,
That wears grief-stricken brow?
When shall the heart make ready
That's dark with sins that cow?
When shall the heart make ready?
The only time is now!

Now let the heart be ready
To call the Saviour in!
Now let the heart be ready,
Jesus will save from sin!
Now let the heart be ready
For God's will triumphing!

The Jubilant

A SOLDIER of the King of kings,
Fighting in The Salvation Army,
Sets his heart on higher things
While fighting in the Army;
And wherever the foe is strongest,
And wherever the fight is longest,
There you will find him jubilant, confident,
On works of mercy and love intent,
Fighting! Fighting! Fighting!
Fighting for the King of kings!

A soldier of the King of kings,
Fighting in The Salvation Army,
Serves his Lord and prays and sings
While fighting in the Army;
And when ground of hope is surest
And the spring of his joy is purest,
Then you will find him jubilant, confident,
On works of mercy and love intent,
Fighting! Fighting! Fighting!
Fighting for the King of kings!

A soldier of the King of kings,
Fighting in The Salvation Army,
Waits on God, mounts up with wings,
While fighting in the Army;
And wherever the way is roughest
And the strife with evil toughest,
There you will find him jubilant, confident,
On works of love and mercy intent,
Fighting! Fighting! Fighting!
Fighting for the King of kings!

What Are These?

[Jesus saith] . . . Lovest thou Me? . . *John* 21:15

WHAT are popularity,
Crowded halls and praise,
All my swift activity,
Moneys that I raise?
Jesus! Jesus! What are these to Thee
If my heart be wandering,
If my love be wavering,
What are these to Thee?

What are eloquence and dash,
Even faithful toil,
All the targets that I smash,
Strongholds I despoil?
Jesus! Jesus! What are these to Thee
If my heart be wandering,
If my love be wavering,
What are these to Thee?

What are promises and prayer,
Courage in the fight,
Sacrifices that I share
In the cause of right?
Jesus! Jesus! What are these to Thee
If my heart be wandering,
If my love be wavering,
What are these to Thee?

A Song About Our Saviour

JESUS Christ the sinner's Saviour,
Jesus Christ the sinner's friend,
Jesus lives and reigns for ever,
Jesus loves us to the end.
Jesus Christ Who saves from sin,
Makes our Heaven and leads us in.

Jesus is our Guide and Brother,
Jesus is our strength and light,
Jesus knows us as no other,
Yet commands to walk in white.
Jesus Christ Who saves from sin,
Sanctifies and keeps us clean.

Jesus, Captain of Salvation,
Calls His soldiers to the fray,
Men of every tribe and nation
He will teach to preach and pray.
Jesus Christ Who saves from sin
Leads us forth to fight and win.

In a dream I heard this sung to the tune Dix, and wrote it on waking.

Prayer For Strength And Time

OH, for the strength of ten
To fight for Christ the Lord;
To rush into the fiercest fray
Wielding His holy sword;
Blow on blow,
Slaying the foe;
Setting free his prey;
Oh, for the strength of ten
Strong and stalwart men
To fight for Christ the Lord!

Oh! for the time of ten
To spend for Christ the Lord;
To take my task from His blessed hands,
Heeding His every word;
Day by day
Doing alway
As my Lord commands;
Oh, for the time of ten
Calm unhurried men
To spend for Christ the Lord!

Retired:
Retrospect And Forecast

. . . when thou shalt be old . . . another shall gird thee, and carry thee whither thou wouldest not. *John* 21:18

The Lord will perfect that which concerneth me. . .
Ps. 138:8

. . . it doth not yet appear what we shall be: but we know that . . . we shall be like Him; for we shall see Him as He is.
1 *John* 3:2

WE have loved and we have chosen,
We have cast the die;
Knowing not what should be woven,
Still the thread we ply.

We have pledged our high endeavour,
Offered all our hours,
Joined ourselves to Christ for ever,
Yielded all our powers.

In the height of youthful ardour
Counted not the cost;
Strong, we only fought the harder
If the day seemed lost.

We have fainted, we have waited,
We have thirsted sore,
Yet with courage unabated
We have striven the more.

And in toiling, fratch and moiling,
Dust of every day,
Kept our motives safe from soiling,
Learned to watch and pray.

We have sown the seed in weakness,
Seen it raised in might,
Suffered foes' assaults with weakness
And have won the fight.

Now, all past shrinks small; time speeding;
Faith alone sees far;
Love dares claim Christ still is leading
Where the ransomed are.

Yes! To old age God will bear us,
Who sustained in youth;
Satan, though he yet may scare us,
Still must fly from truth!

Though the end belie the starting,
Paths we'd rather shun
Opening to us, call for parting
From the joys begun;

When we go whither we would not,
Ruled by others' hands,
If we could evade we must not
Since our God commands!

God, o'er-ruling and perfecting
What doth us concern,
At the last thread's intersecting
Will the pattern turn,

To the shining of Christ's Presence;
Then will leap to view
All time's growth of the soul's essence,
Beauty that God knew!

Likeness to the Lord of Glory!
So divine an end
To our little earthly story
Reason doth transcend!

Love and faith, these can conceive it,
Quickened from on high;
Jesus Christ bids us believe it!
Trusting *Him* we'll die.

And if strength be granted, witness
With our dying breath,
'He is faithful, *now*, Who promised
And hath kept till death.'

THE BEAUTY OF CREATION

The Robin

SILVER bells and running water,
Piping elves and fairies' laughter,
All of these I hear
When the robin dear
Sings his roundelay
At the close of day.

Love of life and all its beauty,
Hope set high for daily duty,
To inspire my heart
Is the robin's part,
As he sings his lay
At the break of day.

My Riches

AND oh, the gold of autumn, the emerald of spring,
The airiness of bird upon the wing;
The flowering meads of summer, the winter's
white and blue,
The wood and dancing waters flowing through;
The hill-top in the morning, the plain at setting
sun,
First glimpse of home and Love when work is done;
The trees, the moors, the rivers, the clouds and
glowing skies,
These all, these all are mine, for I have eyes!

The blackbird's song at twilight, the lark's
delight at dawn,
The whispering in a field of ripening corn;
The sound of mighty waters sighing along the
shore,
The lapwing's call through spring's half-open door;
The bees among the clover, the bells at eventide,
The children's laughter round the fireside;
The wind about the pine-tops, the swallows by the
mere,
These all, these all are mine, for I can hear!

Spring Beauty

OH, beauty! Oh, grace!
Oh, light from God's face!
Are these not for me
Who have eyes to see?

But what if my eyes
Are closed? And the skies
And earth's fair array
Be thus shut away?

Can beauty, can grace,
Can light from God's face
Avail ought to me
Whose eyes *will* not see?

Midsummer Music In England

NO sound discordant, none too low to lend
An added beauty to each voice and blend
Harmoniously with that sweet whole of song
Which makes each day too short, no night too long.
For while earth sends such music to the skies,
Delighted time unfolds his wings and flies!

A Thunder Shower

A FITFUL silence steals upon the wood,
All suddenly the sun's hot rays are fled,
The shining blue of heaven is turned to lead,
Small birds dart by to shelter and the good
Free life of earth is hushed. Gladly I would
Fly too, when swift there falls a light so dread
All turns to dark, and crashing round my head
Roll storms of deafening sound; then rain, a flood!
This we call thunder, and the ancients say
'Tis like the voice of God! But if so, oh!
How shall I bear to hear? Hark! from a spray
Trembling upon the wood's wet rim, the low
Sweet music of a blackbird's simple lay.
Might this not be like to God's voice also?

Summer Rain

OH, God be thanked for gentle summer rain
Which fills the air with dainty points of sound,
And calls the rarest fragrance from the ground
To mingle with the scent of flowers. No grain
Of dust may stay to make its pallid stain
On leaves and little grasses, all are found
Washed over tenderly, and freshly gowned
In all their glowing colours once again.
Yet even summer rain means clouds that spread
About the sky, and shadow everyone,
And some proud beauty's gold and scarlet head
Must bow beneath the drops, its blooming done.
For out of death and darkness life is bred,
And shadows show the glory of the sun.

A Song Of The Seasons

HOW frigidly, how frigidly
The little grasses stand.
How frigidly, how frigidly,
For frost is on the land.
The little streams are still with cold,
The birds are hungry all and bold,
The very twigs, turned hoar and old,
Stand frigidly, oh frigidly,
For frost is on the land;
And frigidly, how frigidly
The little grasses stand.

How daintily, how daintily
The violet grows, and fair.
How daintily, how daintily,
For spring is in the air.
The leaping streams fling wide their song,
The birds fly high and whistle long,
To deck the fields the flowers throng
So daintily, oh daintily,
For spring is in the air;
And daintily, how daintily
The violet grows, and fair.

How busily, how busily
The bee hums to and fro.
How busily, how busily,
For summer's here, you know.
The new-fledged birds begin to fly,
White fleecy clouds go sailing by,
And beauty fills the earth and sky
So busily, oh busily,
For summer's here, you know;
And busily, how busily
The bees hum to and fro.

How quietly, how quietly
Each seed awaits its birth.
How quietly, how quietly,
For rest has come to earth.
The corn uplifts its golden head,
The berries in the sun shine red,
The leaves their russet carpet spread
So quietly, oh quietly,
For rest has come to earth;
And quietly, how quietly
The seeds await their birth.

The Daisy

IN the valley, on the hill,
Close beside the splashing rill,
All across the meadow's face,
Tucked between great stones, like lace
Set about an old grey gown;
Even in the stuffy town
Grows the daisy, gold and white,
What a dear and dainty sprite!

Early on each dewy morn,
When the sunbeams new are born,
The daisy opens wide its eye,
Looking ever to the sky;
Petals all in fresh array,
Head held high to greet the day,
Sets to growing fast and strong,
Keeps on growing all day long.

When the evening's purple robe
Gently spreads about the globe,
Petals of the daisy close
Round its steadfast eye; and those
Near whom prying frost doth glide,
Flush with pride at what they hide.
You may find them, if you seek,
With the blush still on their cheek.

In the valley, on the hill,
Grow the daisies; and they still
Will be growing when I'm gone
Where earth's sun has never shone!
Almost I'd a daisy be,

Have no thoughts but just be free
Lying on earth's bosom; stay
With familiar things alway.

But to know and love are more
Than mere living, and the door
To new beauty stands ajar.
Heav'n is not a land afar!
When man's heart with God is knit,
Then man's life with love is lit;
And his eye, such joys are his,
Sees how fair a daisy is,
Sees by faith a promised land
Made all fair by God's own hand.

The Song

A ROBIN sang one morning,
So merrily sang he.
It set my heart a-singing,
And still sang he.

A robin sang one morning,
So merrily sang he.
It set my heart a-sobbing,
But still sang he!

Larches

A memory of my father in March

BELOVED, the birds are all singing in March,
And always they're singing of you!
See! On the hillside the elegant larch
Wears gown of the soft pale-green hue
That you always would pause to appraise and to
gaze
On the exquisite grace of the tree,
When on the fairest of all the March days,
You chose to go walking with me.

Oh, dear to my memory to see you stand there,
Your eyes like a child's, alight, unaware.

Now, seeing larches in lucent green haze
(And wearing their rubies discreetly!)
Calls my poor heart back to thoughts of March days
(Oh, the birds are singing so sweetly!)
When we would go walking and talking together
To seek out the larches in March,
Agreeing that then, whatever the weather,
No tree is so lovely as larch.

Oh, dear to my memory to see you stand there,
Your eyes like a child's, alight, unaware,
Alight with delight God made larches so fair!

William Bramwell Booth, born 8th March 1856.

I Wonder?

I WAS walking alone among the trees
Listening for a word that they might say,
Listening for the whisper of the breeze,
I wonder, did your thoughts turn that way?

I was walking alone beside the pool,
Mirrored on its face the heavens lay,
Stilly deep the water, clear and cool,
I wonder, did your thoughts turn that way?

I was walking alone toward the hill,
There to see the setting sun's last ray,
That there of space mine eyes might drink their fill,
I wonder, did your thoughts turn that way?

I stood looking afar to distant blue,
Robin, he was singing, he was gay.
Longing seized my heart for sight of you,
I wonder, did your thoughts turn this way?

February

HERE comes fresh February!
And if cold come too,
Clear the skies and nights all starry,
Hoar-frost steals the dew.

Comes February thawing,
Seek for signs of spring,
Violets, and rooks loud cawing,
Stir in everything.

February brings music,
River, brook and rill
Sing and burble, splash and frolic,
As they drink their fill.

February draws posies
Peeping from the ground,
Snowdrops, crocuses, primroses,
Gaily looking round.

In February, rubbish,
Faded end and odd,
Seems to get from sun a burnish
Like a smile from God.

February can entice
Little birds to play,
Finches, dunnocks, wrens and titmice,
Have their saucy say.

Fair February's fragrant,
Crescent moon hangs high,
Robin sings, the happy vagrant,
T'ward west's rosy sky.

February twilight
Flowing from the east
Brings to view, in pleasant foresight,
Rest for man and beast.

Chill February sunrise
Finds the woods still dun,
But each day shows in some new guise,
Winter's on the run!

Welcome, fresh February!
For in any mood
February's salutary
And will do us good.

Early March

THE purpling buds all swelled with rising sap
Are signal each of spring's approach, and though
The sullen winter, loath to go, still wraps
The earth in sudden mist, as if to hide
Her shining bosom; now the warm west wind
Sweeps through the land, seeks out the lingering
snows,
Bids them be gone, and draws with gentle breath
The violet and early primrose forth.
Spring is at hand, and soon all growing things
Will deck themselves for her fair company;
The birds will fill the fragrant air with song,
And even tiny creatures leap for joy,
The land be all alive with ecstasy.

If thou hast eyes to see then, ears to hear,
Go forth and look and listen, worship then
Because thou must, and own God's handiwork.
But if there be a soul one'd with thine own,
Heaven send you opportunity to go
Together through the flowering fields and woods
And up into the hills; for in the spring-time,
Two, wandering so in fresh delight and joy,
Shall meet with God anew, and through the veil
Of beauty spread above, around, beneath,
Perceive the lovely nature of God's mind;
Hear midst surrounding harmonies again
The secret answer of the soul's response,

Spontaneous, certain, clear, that God is love;
His high benevolence the source of joy,
And of the instruments that call joy forth:
Beauty and music and desire; while man,
Attuned by faith to seek and serve his God,
May from His hand receive joy's cup and still
Delighted, thirst again, thus being drawn
In ever clearer confidence to God;
Learn from His love to think His thoughts, as those
Redeemed from sin and fear by Christ shall do,
Seeing creation's beauty from God's side,
Read there the promise of eternal life.

Come lovers, walk together in the spring
And drink again this draught of comfort in.

'. . . Consider The Lilies . . .'

Matt. 6:28

. . . He calleth His own . . . by name. . .
John 10:3

COME, dear one, look on these,
How they do grow,
And trust our Father's love
Who made them so.

Come, let us trust His care,
Who, for its hour,
Hath made so wondrous fair
The fading flower.

Shall He not then much more
Adorn thy soul,
Prepare it here for Love's
Eternal goal?

Let us His wisdom trust
Who knows our frame,
Who made us from the dust,
Who calls our name.

Come, dear one, look on these
And trust God's love
To make thee perfect fair
For life above.

Written for a friend and sent to her with flowers when she lay dying.

May Morning

Rain before seven, fine by eleven. *Country Saying*

THE silent morning swathed in grey
Creeps stealthily abroad,
With downcast eyes she takes her way
Over the dusky sward.
The sleepy birds delay their song
And morning falls to sighing,
Decides she'll do the day a wrong,
Then sets to gently crying.

Oh, fickle-fair! When day appears
Expecting to be sad,
She doffs her grey, laughs off her tears
And tells him to be glad!

Who would not joy to see her stand
All radiant blue and white,
Smiling upon the fragrant land
Her tears have made all bright?
Day will forgive her, so will I,
Moods raising false alarms,
For tears in morning's laughing eyes
But add to morning's charms.

Butterfly In July

I SAW pure beauty animate in light,
A 'Silver Blue' in first ecstatic flight
Above a sea of carmine heather bell,
As though uncertain, featherlike there fell
From cloudless heaven a flake of deeper blue,
Delicious contrast to the glowing hue
Of the sun-reddened spray to which it clings,
Sipping sweet nectar, spreading azure wings.
I paused, on loveliness to feast my eyes,
Felt then my soul get glimpse of paradise –
That God, so strong in power, should want to make
This passing scene just for its beauty's sake!
Thought quickened awesome in my mind that He
Must want to make a lovelier thing of me!

October Gold

. . . the morning stars sang together, and all the sons of God shouted for joy. *Job* 38:7

OH! Have you seen the gold come in, in October?
The gorgeous, gaudy, grandly glowing gold!
And do you know, some say, they like tones more sober?
Infer the gold is merely leaves grown old!

But if you've seen October gold in its glory,
You know an artist's mind has made it so;
You *know* it's not just lack of sap, leaves grown hoary,
But beauty planned in all that golden glow.

So when I see October gold, I go singing,
As sons of God and morning stars may do
When they behold God's perfect works good, and bringing
A token that He cares for me and you.

For God has made things beautiful in their season,
And giv'n men sight, a mind that apprehends;
With joy of heart confirmed in them by sweet reason,
That God is power, Who all His works transcends.

Oh! I have seen the gold come in, in October!
And God Himself the glory of the gold,
Promising life, when my brief spell here is over,
A hint my spirit never shall grow old!

November

IN November bitter sweet,
Spring and winter meet.
On the soft salubrious days
Gorgeous sun rides in through haze,
Girdles earth with pink and gold,
Spreads out colour fold on fold;
Then, November rivals May
In rich brilliance of array;
Yellows, crimsons, lushy browns,
Purple-blue on distant downs,
Lemon stubble fields and green,
Each with hedgerow drawn between,
Traced about with filigree,
Hazel, hawthorn, and a tree
Solitary here and there
Hedgers had a mind to spare.
These lines all are splashed with red
Till the hungry birds are fed;
Or, grey-swathed in trav'ller's rest,
Touched with scarlet at the crest
By white bryony's burnished berries,
Like a small child's size in cherries.
Corn is then all harvested;
But remain unmolested
Late ripe blackberries and sloes,
Blue-bloomed loveliness that grows
Thick-set on the slender branches,
Beauty setting sun enhances,
Touching lingering leaf to gold
As cock pheasant's call rings bold!

In November may be heard
Gentle singing of blackbird,
As if he were conning o'er
Phrases he'd not sung before;
Or, as though whilst half asleep,
Memories of last spring he'd keep.
Thrush sings in another key,
Quite authoritatively
He lays down the law and shouts,
'Do it! Do it!' Never doubts
He'll be king in his domain
When the spring comes round again.
But of songsters in November
Robin is my favourite member;
Mournfully he sometimes sings,
Hesitates to use his wings,
Hops about close to the ground
But his song's a lovely sound
Sad or gay; even in fog
Perched upon a fallen log
Robin's singing casts a spell,
Brings me thoughts I cannot tell.

Raucous on the tranquil air
Pheasant's cry warns hare to lair
As November's monster moon
Rising in late afternoon
Smiling dons a robe of yellow,
Jolly incandescent fellow.
Soon the stubble field flows white
To the verge of wood's black night
Where the trees stand still as death,
Till a little breeze draws breath,
Then goes wandering away
Letting the still silence stay.
One day comes a stronger breeze
Passing by the fringe of trees,
Sighs in gusts then with a whine

Leaps among the tops of pine,
While the clouds move in procession
Past the moon to take possession
Of the heaven, far and wide,
Till they shut the moon outside!
Then the winds come sweeping in
And November gales begin.
There's a grandeur in their clangour,
Howls whose sound seems full of rancour,
Limbs of mighty trees are taken
In the storm's stern grip and shaken
Till the tree, it seems, must split
Or crash down in midst of it.
Dry leaves driven high, the rain
Weighs them down to earth again,
Rain, that hissing, stings and beats
Through the now deserted streets,
Adding to the tumult's roar
Thundering at every door;
While at sea the mighty deeps
Heave and press and rise in heaps.
As the storm drives on and leaves
Stricken ships, stripped tiles and eaves,
Dawn will bring the saddening sight
Of great elm or pine, its height
Seeming higher, as it lies
Prostrate, never more to rise!

Come surprises in November
As had spring-time's dying ember
Suddenly flared up and shone
With a grace we thought had gone
When the summer came to stay.
It might happen any day!
Then the heaven above, blue bright,
Fills the woods with gentle light;
Rhododendron's burnished green
Makes a background for this scene.

All the silent glade lies sleeping
When comes flashing, tumbling, leaping,
Brilliant brimstone butterfly:
Catches then and keeps my eye.
Instantly the glade's awake
As that bright flake swoops to take
Rest, a very jewel of light,
Wide-winged on dark leaf, a sight
Memory will cherish long.
Only absence of bird song
Tells me spring's not in the air,
This November day's so fair!

Yet the evening may turn chill
As through lowland, up the hill,
Frost and fog creep on together;
Then we learn the vilest weather
May set in and prove November
Darker, colder than December!
In the cities mid-day dark,
In the country opaque dark,
Suffocating pall that hides
Earth and skies and all besides.
Rumours somehow rise and run
From the tip of every tongue!
Milk-van upside-down in lane!
Hundreds waiting for the train
Shivering at the local station!
Sneezing seizes the whole nation!
Frost on roads brings icy patches,
Fog holds up the football matches!
Don't complain too much, remember,
After all this is November.

December

DECEMBER?
Oh, as I remember December,
December's very fair,
With a bitter sweet tang in the air
And the sun going down solid crimson,
Quite close to the horizon.
And at night, riding high
In an indigo sky,
Snow white the moon!
While by day the bare birch woods wait pinkish maroon,
And so far as eye reaches
Stand oaks, elms and beeches,
Their delicate forms, as of all unrobed trees,
Etched black on the sky; and down on the lees
The cattle drift by, belly high in mist,
As the evening turns grey from amethyst.
Soon stars are shining incredibly bright,
Oh the glory of a December night!
Now cold creeps up to curtained window
And drowsy child snuggles close to pillow,
While downstairs fires glow and leap
And grown-ups talk to postpone sleep.
Yes! And sometimes in December,
I remember,
Waking to the solemn silence,
Prelude to muffled sound's quiescence,
That heralds in a world robed white –
So white, that even on a moonless night
There shimmers a soft glow

To show the lovely face of snow.
Then when sun is shining,
Or, rosy red, declining,
The snow's all sparkling,
And pine, that winter darkling,
Stands decked with diamonds reflecting
Light from every facet, unsuspecting
Its bright ephemeral beauty, shadowed blue;
Surely *that* was made for you?
And surely someone's eyes were meant to see
The beauty of a holly tree
Freshly adorned with snow?
Else none would know
How scarlet bright its berry,
None feel the heart grow merry
At the thought God made it
Just like that, and gave it
Free to you and me
Just to make us happy!
And blessed Christmas Day comes in December,
When men with joy remember
How God our King came down
To little Bethlehem's town,
To save us all
From Satan's thrall;
And waits sing
And church bells ring
On holy Christmas Eve,
Bidding us all afresh believe afresh receive
Our Saviour, Christ the Lord,
And joy in His life-giving word.
Oh, happiest hopes are in the air
And . . . yes! December's very fair
As *I* remember
December.

Sweet Briar In Suffolk

A little fantasia

OH, meet
The briar should be sweet
That once was plaited to a crown of thorns
And pressed
In cruel jest
Upon His brow Whom now the whole world
  mourns:
For in that dear propinquity its stems
Became bedewed with crimson drops like gems,
And thorn pricks there began the precious flow
That washes scarlet sins as white as snow!
Yes, meet
The briar should be sweet
That still was wound about His kingly head
When from the cross His friends received Christ
  dead.
Gently they disengaged those thorns, nor thought
Their Lord a little miracle of love had wrought
When He was slain and His dear body broken.
He gave those thorns new fragrant life in token
That they had touched Him then, and hence,
Like incense,
The briar a sweet aroma spreads: a legacy to me
From dear Christ dying on the tree.
Oh, meet
The briar should be sweet
And wear its gems blood red
To mind me of my Saviour dying
With thorns about His head.

Thinking About Roses

HOW long would it take to thank God for the rose?
The exquisite wild rose that blooms in hedgerows,
The delicate tea rose all fragrance that blows
In sunny south lands where the great river flows,
Oh, I should like to thank God for all those!

How long would it take to thank God for the rose?
The dear garden roses, some fit for flower shows,
The old ones with names that now nobody knows!
And the elegant new ones in colour that glows,
Oh, I should like to thank God for all those!

How long would it take to thank God for the rose?
For climbers and bushes, the moss rose I chose
That still in odd corners of old gardens grows,
For bright little dwarf ones they plant out in rows,
Oh, I should like to thank God for all those!

Yet from when I begin to the time of life's close,
Would not be enough time to thank God for the
rose,
The beautiful, fragrantly, long-blooming rose!
But I hold to the hope Christ Jesus gives me
Of a life after death, from time's bondage free.
And oh! What a heavenly joy it will be
To thank God for the loveliness we call the rose!

The West Wind

THE west wind is blowing!
New impulses of life run through the land.
The west wind is blowing!
Fresh beauty now prepares at God's command.
The west wind is blowing!
The violets are smiling in their sleep.
The west wind is blowing!
The hazel catkins swinging dance and leap.
The west wind is blowing!
The chill north lands are turning toward the sun,
January's nearly over, spring's begun!
Blowing high, blowing low, the west wind is
blowing!

The Holly Tree

OH, God be praised for the holly tree!
The beautiful shining holly tree!
In spring-time its blossoms milk-white deck the
trees,
Providing a feast for all manner of bees;
The humming they make's a delicious sound
As it drifts through the fragrant air around
The flowering holly tree,
Whose leaves are so cunningly fashioned and
burnished,

They sparkle and glow as though they were
furnished
With light of their own! And they wear for
protection
Sharp prickles protruding in every direction;
Oh, prickly fair holly tree!
But winter's the time when the holly tree
Puts on her jewels for all to see;
Bright scarlet berries on slender green stems,
Oh, lovely is holly when wearing her gems;
Most beautiful holly tree!

Yes! I am glad for the holly tree,
The beautiful shining holly tree!
It lifts up my thoughts to eternity,
And adds to the joys of Heaven for me,
For when I'm there I shall really see
The Maker of the holly tree!
The beautiful shining holly tree!

The Flower Garden

I KNOW a summer garden
Full of beautiful things,
I know a summer garden
Where the blackcap sings;
I know a summer garden
Where there are roses and pinks,
A dear little summer garden
Where the wild bee drinks.

I know an autumn garden
Bright with butterflies' wings,
I know an autumn garden
Where frost changes things;
I know an autumn garden
Dahlias and michies and all
Sink to sleep in this dear garden
As the pale leaves fall.

I know a winter garden
Hollies shield from the north,
I know a winter garden
Snowdrops there spring forth;
I know a winter garden
Fieldfares and redwings come there
To feed in this winter garden
Finding winter fare.

I know a spring-time garden
Robins come there for fun,
I know a spring-time garden
Warm in rising sun;
I know a spring-time garden
Pale yellow brimstone knows too
And finds in this spring-time garden
Blooms of ev'ry hue.

I know this flower garden
Love has walked there with me,
Looked to a wide horizon
Far as eyes can see;
Looked to the dome of heaven,
Glorious by day and by night,
From this dear flower garden
Place of pure delight.

IN SORROW AND IN JOY

A Question

OH! The pain of sorrow!
It robs hope of tomorrow,
Lends a light to yesterday,
Casts a shadow all the way
The heavy heart must tread,
Longing for its dead,
Hungry for that shining past
Suddenly estranged, and cast
Beyond the desert waste,
Which instantly effaced
The happy present.
Say,
Can time steal such pain away?
Heal the wounds of sorrow,
Give hope back tomorrow?

Let Christ Jesus Heal

. . . and with His stripes we are healed.
Isa. 53:5

ART thou poor, forlorn, and lost,
Wearied from a fruitless seeking?
Hast spent all to pay the cost
Of a pleasure ever fleeting?
Bow thy head and bare thy heart,
Let Christ Jesus heal thy smart!

Art thou stained by any sin,
Captive to a fleshly passion?
Doth thy soul at length begin
To bemoan its earthly fashion?
Bow thy head and bare thy heart,
Let Christ Jesus heal thy smart!

Doth thy thirst for righteousness
Turn all other good to ashes?
Doth despair turn prophetess,
As thy springing hope she dashes?
Bow thy head and bare thy heart,
Let Christ Jesus heal thy smart!

Doth past failure still pursue
And deride thee, who art burning
With a shame that doth renew
All thy pain and fruitless yearning?
Bow thy head and bare thy heart,
Let Christ Jesus heal thy smart!

Let Christ Jesus heal thy smart,
Thou'lt not find a touch more tender,
Nor 'gainst sin to take thy part
Find more valiant a Defender.
Bow thy head and bare thy heart,
Jesus Christ will heal thy smart.

Uninvited

March 1928

SHE did not wait to be invited,
But stepped inside my door
Whilst I was busy getting ready
To welcome joy once more:
She merely looked at me and whispered,
'Joy will not come today.'
I looked at her, and then I knew
Sorrow had come to stay.

On Any Day To A Friend

OH, I have been so happy
On many a day like this,
When your endearing presence
Has filled my cup with bliss.

Has filled my cup with bliss
To hear your voice once more,
And it would make me happy now
As on many a day before.

As on many a day before
When we walked toward the hill,
Where but for time's exigencies,
We might be walking still.

We might be walking still
Where the mighty beeches grow,
Or over the high ridge to view
The land spread out below.

The land spread out below,
The green field and the corn,
The lovely land of England
Where you and I were born.

Where you and I were born,
Her hills and vales and trees,
Her gently flowing rivers,
Shores washed by seven seas.

Shores washed by seven seas,
Refreshed by wind and rain,
With mist in the fragrant hollows
Till sunshine come again.

Till sunshine come again
Where you and I have met
To keep a tryst with sorrow
With hopes we can't forget.

With hopes we can't forget,
With songs we cannot sing,
And there Love came to meet us
And shined on everything.

And shined on everything,
The future and the past,
And made a feast in paradise
Of what had been a fast.

Of what had been a fast,
Love made a happy day,
A place of peace and innocence
Where we could praise and pray.

Where we could praise and pray,
On many a day like this,
When your endearing presence
Has filled my cup with bliss,
Has filled my cup with bliss
On many a day like this.

Song for Grandchildren To Sing

DARLING Grandma hear us sing,
Joy be yours today;
Heaven smile on everything,
Give you joy today.
We your children's children pray
God to bless you on your way,
And from loving hearts we say,
Joy be yours today!

Refrain
Joy be yours!
All your children's children say,
Joy be yours today!

Happy secrets are in store
For your joy today,
May your hopes for us make more
Joy for you today:
That we all are growing strong
In the fight for right 'gainst wrong,
That we each to Christ belong
Be your joy today!

Grief

GRIEF is ever old!
Though mine came but yesterday.
Tarnished's all my gold;
Faded all my treasure.
Joy the fair lies dead
In a past already dim,
Dust about her head,
Silenced all her laughter.

Grief is ever old!
Ever new, its bitter smart
Turns all comfort cold,
Dooms all hope to wither.
Sun and stars forgot,
Grief's cold shadow over all;
Life's once pleasant plot
Desolate lies and ravished.

Grief is ever old!
All the fair familiar things
To its bondage sold,
Serve to feed its vigour.
Time's slow march of days,
Each must bow to grief's hard yoke;
Nowhere quiet ways
Free from its drear presence.

Grief is ever old!
Ever present, ever dumb,
Never can be told
Half grief brings of sorrow.
There remains but death,
Strong enough it seems to slay,
By its icy breath,
Time and grief together.

To My Father

LIKE the music of the water flowing ever through the wood,
Is the thought of all thy tenderness, the thought of all thy good:
It gives my heart a happiness no other music could,
Like the music of the water flowing ever through the wood.

Like the music of the water when the birds are singing high,
When the wind is in the tree tops and the leaves all twist and sigh,
So the memory of thy care for me sounds on and very nigh,
Like the music of the water in the wood still flowing by.

Like the music of the water when the storm is loud
and shrill,
Making sweeter to my spirit days when peace
the woods did fill,
In grief the music in my heart tells of thy dear
goodwill,
Like the music of the water in the wood unsilenced
still.

The Suffolk Coast, After My Father's Death

. . . the time of the singing of birds is come. . .
S. of S. 2:12

THE larks are singing in all this lovely land
Where the grass grows down to the sea;
Where the gorse spreads golden to the cliff's sheer
edge
And there's blackthorn and hawthorn in every
hedge,
And oh! What memories for me!

The larks are singing in all this lovely land;
But my heart is heavy as lead:
When I walk the sea shore, or the flow'ring lees,
Or on common or heathland, or close 'neath the
trees;
Anywhere; everywhere; for he is not there,
Though the land that he loved lies smiling fair. . .
For oh, my Beloved lies dead,
And my heart is heavy as lead;
While the larks are singing in all this lovely land
Where the grass grows down to the sea.

Rest In This

REST in this, poor heart: God knows
All thy fears,
All the questions they impose,
All the tears.
Knowing all, He still doth say,
'Child! Trust in Me today.'

Rest in this, poor heart: God sees
All thy grief,
All the fruitless search for ease,
For relief.
Seeing all, He still doth say,
'Child! Trust in Me today.'

Rest in this, poor heart: God hears
Satan's plea,
Who by promises or jeers
Tempteth thee.
Hearing all, He still doth say,
'Child! Trust in Me today.'

The Listening Ear

I will hear what God the Lord will speak: for He will speak. . .
Ps. 85:8

I LOVE the wide grey stretches of the skies,
Where I may look afar, and rest my eyes.
I love the blessed silence, where I hear
The gentle sounds that soothe my weary ear.
I love the cool, hard earth, where I may lie
And stretch my aching limbs, and feel the shy
Caress of summer breeze upon my cheek,
And wait, unhurried, for the Lord to speak.

I love the noise of battle and the sound
Of clashing arms: 'tis there I would be found!
I love to share the desperate, daring fight
That men must make who choose to walk in white.
I love to plunge into the fiercest fray,
That hand and head and heart of mine may play
Their part for God. For there my soul shall hear
His voice, than all the battle's din more clear.

For so it is with God! If He but find
The listening ear, He will make known His mind;
Be heard as clearly 'midst life's multitude
As in the calm of leisured solitude.
For me what matters is that I should hear,
In peace or war, His voice, and only fear
Lest selfish joy or doubting care should be
My confidant, when God would speak to me.

My Mother's Voice

THE sound of my dear one's voice to me
Is like the sound of a summer sea
When it softly sighs along the shore,
Full of memories of days before –
So is the voice of my Love to me.

The sound of my dear one's voice to me
Is like the whisper of wind to tree
When the leaves sing back their point of sound
Fresh to the sun-parched earth around –
So is the voice of my Love to me.

The sound of my dear one's voice to me
Is like the sound of sweet minstrelsy
When it grandly soars, or with swift surprise
Falls to tenderness, music-wise –
So is my Mother's voice to me.

The sound of my dear one's voice to me
Is all that I say and more, since she,
Beyond the music, her love doth tell,
New to my heart that knows it well;
Oh, delight of her voice to me!

Where Shall I Weep?

OH! Where shall I weep for my Beloved,
Where shall I weep?

In the places he loved, there weep for him,
For never more shall his fair presence grace them.
Go! find in the wild sweet of Dartmoor's hills
And close beside her leaping waters
The little wandering paths he knew, and trace them
To the dear spots he chose, where never more
The music of his voice shall make complete
For thee the harmonies of nature's playing.
There shalt thou weep for thy Beloved,
Weep sore.

Oh! When shall I weep for my Beloved,
When shall I weep?

When thou art alone; then weep for him,
Hiding from those who love him too thine anguish.
When morning blushes light the eastern sky
And larks wake day in happy chorus:
Be listening then, while sleep-born hopes all
languish anguish.
No dawn, however fair, no lark's glad song
Shall herald his approach on earth again
Whom thou hast loved and lost: alone, at dawn,
Then shalt thou weep for thy Beloved,
Weep long.

Sorrow In Spring

I USED to think the singing of the birds in spring
One of earth's sweetest sounds:
To hear the night's soft breathing hushed for
listening
As up the lark rose flinging to the skies his song
For the very joy of singing, used to be among
Life's dearly treasured joys.
But now, I find the singing of the birds in spring
One of earth's saddest sounds:
To hear the robin whistling, or the willow wren
Scatter his silver warbling 'mong the leaves, or
when
The nightingale is filling all the night with peace
As though the joy of loving never more would
cease,
Wakes all my heart to pain.

For all the lovely singing of the birds in spring
Tells me I never more
Shall rise to meet his coming whom my heart holds
dear:
No morning, no! nor evening, find the loved one
near.
The birds will go on singing as when he and I
Together walked communing with earth and sea
and sky.
Singing, singing, singing –
All the birds in spring,
And I must hear them sing.

Faith Comes

HOPE lies dying:
Sun is sinking in the west,
Dark clouds vying
With up-stealing night to spread
Darkness over all,
Darkness for hope's pall,
Hiding all the flowers.
Birds in their bowers
Shiver and creep closer,
Darkness growing grosser
Shuts the very heavens out,
Closes in and round about,
Almost stifles breath
While life awaits hope's death:
For if hope be dead,
All of life is said.

Will hope die?
No! At midnight
Comes a cry,
Comes a glow-worm light,
Comes faith walking in the dark.
Faintest gleam her footsteps mark;
Faith's voice praying low,
Faith's voice singing low;
Pitchy blackness all around,
Save where faith's feet touch the ground,
Faith can see by that dim glow
The right next step to go.
Memory and the law, faith brings,
To sustain her as she sings.

Faith, though trembling, yet is bold:
Faith can wait and not grow cold.
And while faith her watch is keeping
Sinking hope lies gently sleeping.
Then faith turns her seeing eyes
To the darkened eastern skies.
Presently,
Silently,
In the blackest lack of light
Is the dark heart of the night
Arrowed through by palest ray,
Promise of hope's living day.

Hope's not dying,
Sleeping, sighing,
At day-break
Hope will wake!

My Saviour's Voice

I LOVE the sound of my Saviour's voice
When He bids my heart rejoice;
I love the touch of my Saviour's hand
When He leads me into a promised land;
But the depth and height of His love to me
I only dimly begin to see,
When in the dark of a sorrow's night,
I lean on Him and feel His might;
And I taste how tender and strong and true
Is His love to the weak like me and you;
When a storm is raging and terror near,
He whispers so that my heart can hear
'Fear not, my child, for thou art dear.'

Oh! I love the sound of my Saviour's voice
And it makes my heart rejoice.

Question And Answer

HAS hope anything to say?
Quiet! Hope lies sleeping;
Longing heart, don't wake her pray,
Joys are in her keeping;
For if hope should waken, they
And sweet hope might go away.

The Past That Might Have Been

DULL, dismal, desolate days,
When thrusting thought incessant plays
Regret's refrain,
And at the end
Begins again.
And then
Again begins the poignant pain
Of seeing things that might have been.
Begins again
To that refrain
And pain
The stinging smart of seeing
Pass, without being,
All pageant-like before the mind's clear eye,
The beautiful unseen
That might have been.
All pageant-like before the mind's clear eye,

The beautiful unborn I mourn goes by.
The beautiful and bravely lovely,
By the world unseen.
The beautiful, the bravely lovely,
The past that might have been!

Solace

WHAT if my heart be
Burdened and guilty,
Could Christ give release?
Yes, if confessing
Thy sin and repenting,
Give thee peace.

Refrain
Give thee peace:
Christ the Lord will give thee peace,
Heal thy wounds, pardon all thy sin
And give thee peace.

If I should need Him,
If I should seek Him,
Should I find Him near?
Yes, if thou seek Him
In truth, thou shalt find Him,
Find Him here.

If I should follow
What of tomorrow,
Would Christ show the way?
Yes, He will guide thee,
Himself walk beside thee,
Every day.

Oh, Glad The Day

OH, sad the day
When to my unlatched door came sin,
Who straight a stirring tale did spin
Of pleasure; said, 'Shall I come in,
And let thee taste the sweet
Of this, my meat?'
And I said, 'Yea.'

Oh, sad the day
When conscience whispered, 'Bid sin go!
Art sleeping, that thou dost not know
How swiftly sin is wont to grow?
He'll master thee! Have done!
Bid him be gone!'
But I said, 'Nay.'

Oh, sad the day
When to my happy, simple feast
With innocence, sin brought a beast.
Then laughed and said, 'Thou must at least
Acknowledge he's thy kin.
Come, let him in!'
And I said, 'Yea.'

Oh, sad the day
When in the greying dawn remorse
Tapped at the lattice, said in hoarse,
Harsh voice, 'Turn out the beast by force!'
But fear lest sin should wake
Did make me quake,
And I said, 'Nay.'

Oh, sad the day
When sin said, 'Up! Drive off dull care,
Forget thy dreams, and let us share
Excitement such as devils dare!
Are thoughts not with thee yet
Thou wouldst forget?'
And I said, 'Yea.'

Oh, sad the day
When One I fain would open for
Approached. I longed now to implore
His entrance, but sin barred the door,
Sneered, 'What! To this foul den?'
I trembled then,
And answered, 'Nay!'

Oh, glad the day
That saw Him on my threshold stand.
The gulf 'twixt Him and me love-spanned
When knocking with His wounded hand
He said, 'Wilt let Me in?
I save from sin!'
And I said, 'Yea.'

Though Tossed By Temptation

. . . our Saviour, and Lord Jesus Christ . . . is our hope.
1 *Tim.* 1:1

[Jesus said] As the Father hath loved me, so have I loved you. . . *John* 15:9

THOUGH tossed by temptation
I need not despair,
There's hope of Salvation
For souls everywhere,
While Jesus, our Saviour,
His love doth declare,
I need not, I dare not, I will not despair.

Though doubting and fearing,
I need not despair,
For God still is hearing
The penitent's prayer,
While Jesus, our Saviour,
His love doth declare,
I need not, I dare not, I will not despair.

There's promise of power
I need not despair,
There's grace for each hour
All trial to bear,
While Jesus, our Saviour,
His love doth declare,
I need not, I dare not, I will not despair.

This can be sung to the tune O Boundless Salvation

Tears

SOMETIMES it seems that I have never wept,
So many of love's tears unshed within my heart I've kept.
So many memories there like shrouded pictures dark and still,
Until some new-born joy or grief awake in me the will
To look again on scenes long past;
Then fall my tears, fall fast.

But We See Jesus

. . . Fear not . . . I have called thee by thy name; thou art mine. *Isa.* 43:1

WHEN sickness comes and all my plans lie shattered,
When praying seems to be of no avail,
When to get well, I felt, was all that mattered,
When even love no longer could prevail:
Then,
Jesus I see!
And He speaks to me,
He tells me His love is the same
In sickness or health,
Privation or wealth,
He loves me! He knows me by name!

When hope must hear again the word deferred,
When dreams of joy fade out into the night,
When fears surround and closer creep unheard,
When I stare into dark and see no light:
Then,
Jesus I see!
And He speaks to me,
He tells me His love is the same
In sickness or health,
Privation or wealth,
He loves me! He knows me by name!

When health returns and hopes dance in my heart,
When joy streams in like sunshine after rain,
When love resumes her throne and plays her part,
When faith lights all my way to life again:
Then,
Jesus I see!
And He speaks to me,
He tells me His love is the same
In sickness or health,
Privation or wealth,
He loves me! He knows me by name!
He loves me! He knows me by name!

Mary Magdalene

. . . call His Name Jesus: for He shall save His people from their sins. *Matt.* 1:21

PAUPER in all but tears,
Of all but love deplete,
I still may overcome my fears,
Still wash Thy feet.

Still, love may do her part,
Still reverently touch,
Anoint Thee, Who to my poor heart
Hast forgiv'n much.

Still in the sight of man,
I may with tears adore,
However dark my sin, I can
Still love Thee more.

More than the pharisee,
Who never felt his shame
Cry to remind Thy purity,
'Jesus!' Thy Name.

More than the righteous rich,
Who never gave Thee kiss,
Yet O my heart we know to which
Thou saidst, 'Go in peace!'

And still through earth's sad lands,
Where Satan has his seat,
Sinners, with tears and loving hands
May wash Christ's feet!

Peter

And the Lord turned, and looked upon Peter. And Peter remembered the word of the Lord. . . *Luke* 22:61

POOR Peter thrice denied,
Thrice cried,
'I know Him not!'

Peter, poor craven, in the chill of night,
Stood warming himself at the fire light,
His Master's word forgot:
Until Christ Jesu turned His eyes
To look on him! Then, Peter flies
Weeping out into the cold night's dark.
But there's no dark can hide the mark,
The spreading blot that came
On Peter's heart
When he denied his Master's name;
Denied and cried,
'I know Him not!'

Peter, who thrice denied,
Must see how died
The Lamb of God!

Weak Peter, boasting, 'Lord, though all forsake,
Yet will not I!' He could not wake
While his dear Master trod
Anguished, alone, His path in prayer;
Bowed in His grief, submitting there
To drink the appointed cup, to meet
Betrayal by kiss. The traitor's feet
With malice shod,

Found the accustomed place.
Judas! His heart so base
He could sell innocence,
Gave Jesus to His foes, and hence
Poor Peter saw Him taken, saw Him slain,
Saw Christ's blood flow and stain
The inoffensive earth.
Peter, whose fears gave birth
To that thrice-made denial,
Stands by the Cross, himself on trial;
His own accusing heart condemns to sorrow
His past, his present and each new tomorrow!
Peter, who thrice denied, must hear
His own voice ever in his ear,
Must feel hope stifled by regret
That mounts in him like unpaid debt.

Poor Peter who denied;
At Calvary sees how died
The Son of God!

. . . Peter was grieved because [Jesus] said unto him the third time, Lovest thou me? And he said unto Him, Lord, Thou knowest all things; Thou knowest that I love Thee. . .

John 21:17

Yet he who thrice denied
Thrice cried,
'Lord, I love Thee!'

As seven disciples in the chill of dawn
(His dripping cloak round Peter drawn)
Sit close about a fire on the shore,
Poor Peter hears Christ Jesu's voice once more,
Asking, 'Dost thou love Me?'
And Peter's eyes leap up to flash
Love, even shame cannot abash,
Straight to Christ's eyes, and mutely plead
In penitential worship all his need.

And now all eyes on Peter turn,
See mount his brow, there burn
Memory's hot blush for those base moments
When he denied his Lord; nor guessed the torments
Lying in hiding in his deed
Like dormant seed
Ready to spring in riotous succession forth,
A poisonous weed to choke all flowers of worth;
For cowardice in prospect's sure of camouflage,
'Tis afterwards the deed breaks forth an outrage,
Making the night's sweet silence one long shout
To which the swelling pulse beats out
The inner anguish of regret,
The passionate wishing to undo, unmet!

Peter who knew all this, broke silence,
Speaking with eager cadence,
'Lord, I *love* Thee!'
And, still his eyes on Christ intent,
A little t'ward Him bent,
As though to cast himself at Jesu's feet,
His declaration to repeat.
Then, 'Feed My lambs,' Christ said,
And while poor Peter's eyes still pled,
Clear called the question once again,
'Simon, dost thou love Me?'

Wincing as from a blow in pain,
His eyes still fixed on Christ's in supplication,
Peter repeats his love's asseveration,
'Yea, Lord, Thou knowest that I love Thee!'
Swift answer, 'Feed My sheep!'
And Christ's eyes Peter's keep.
The question He renews
As though He'd heard no answer and would use
The words thrice spoken
As held they secret token
'Twixt Him and Peter!
Then paled poor Peter's cheek,

Lips parting as to speak,
But fear choked in his throat
The torrent of his words, and smote
Upon his heart despairing knell:
How could the same lips tell
His love to Jesus, that had thrice denied?
That had with curses lied,
'I know Him not'?

His gaze still Jesu's eyes updrinking,
As could he there lay bare Christ's thinking,
Peter sits motionless, tense, dumb,
As had his heart been frozen numb.

And now the silence speaks along the beach;
And may not silence lie as well as speech?

Poor Peter, looking still on Christ,
Feels suddenly his heart un-iced,
Feels surging joy unseal his tears,
Swift, sweep away his fears,
Powerless, in face of this dear truth: *Christ knows
What is in man!* Words are not needed to disclose
Poor heart's possession,
Nor groans for intercession!
All that the lips could tell
The Saviour knows full well.
Oh, hope! Oh, happiness!
Oh, soul restoring tenderness,
Christ Jesus knows it all,
The boasts, the fears, the fall!
Knows too, the love that fills poor Peter's breast,
The longing to fulfil his Lord's behest,
And looking steadfast in Christ's eyes
Peter in rapture cries:
'My Lord, Thou knowest all things.'
(Ah! Confident, poor Peter's voice now rings)
'Thou *knowest* that I love Thee!'
Then, 'Feed my sheep, and one day die for me,'

The Lord replied,
And thus poor Peter who had thrice denied,
By Jesu's mercy thrice his love declared!
And dared,
In Satan's spite, who him would claim,
In face of friends who knew his shame,
Lift up his eyes and look
On Jesus Christ, Whom he forsook:
Lift up his eyes and joyful take
Command to live and die for Jesu's sake.

Oh! Happy Peter,
Once a traitor,
Now forgiven. Restored
To love's eternal friendship with his Lord!

Love In Exile

THAT'S all ended! What a pity!
Love that promised fair,
Long before its full bloom beauty,
Wilted in the alien air.
Only one thing could be sadder:
That love should have flourished there!

Little Love's Tale

. . . God is love. . . 1 *John* 4:16

[Jesus said] . . . Come and see. . . *John* 1:39

. . . I will . . . sup with him, and he with me. *Rev.* 3:20

LOVE said to love, 'Come and see!'
But fear cried out shrill,
'No! It bodes us ill!'
Still,
LOVE said 'Come!'

LOVE said to love, 'Come and see!'
And fear sighed 'Beware,
Thou'lt be censured there!'
Still,
LOVE said 'Come!'

LOVE said to love, 'Come and see!'
Then fear sneered, 'No doubt
Hope will be cast out!'
Still,
LOVE said 'Come!'

Still,
LOVE said to love, 'Come and see!'
So love ran to LOVE,
Looked in the eyes of LOVE,
Saw there only LOVE,
Found new life in LOVE,
Found that fear had fled,
All on which fear fed
LOVE'S omnipotence

Turned to confidence;
Full trust in LOVE'S power
Blossomed like a flower
In love's mind, and gave
LOVE the chance to save.

LOVE, Almighty LOVE!
LOVE, Infinite LOVE!
Drew love up,
Little love to sup!

Love said to LOVE, 'Let me stay,
Feast or fast, first, last,
Through joy, through grief, past
Tempest, hope and loss,
Past pains, past gains: count dross
All life that is not love answering to LOVE!
LOVE!
Let me stay!'

LOVE answered, 'At My side,
Love may evermore abide!'

'Therefore now
Seest thou,
Love alive to LOVE,
Love at rest in LOVE,
Still
Loving LOVE.'

Let Us Love

Beloved, let us love . . . for love is of God. . . 1 *John* 4:7

[Jesus said] . . . It is more blessed to give than to receive.
Acts 20:35

BELOVED, let us love!
For where there's love there's life!
There's life and all love's exquisite enjoyment
Shedding a glow on all our time's employment.
Beloved, let us love!

Beloved, let us love!
For where there's love there's joy!
Love's joy in loving, and love's joy in giving,
Which love soon learns is more than all receiving.
Beloved, let us love!

Beloved, let us love!
For where there's love there's comfort!
Comfort in grief, in daily trials balm,
In midst of storm love's there, courageous, calm.
Beloved, let us love!

Beloved, let us love!
For love is born of God!
His mark hid in each heart, by His help growing
Till likeness to Himself shall through our flesh
be showing.
Beloved, let us love!

Beloved, let us love!
Love more; for God is love!
And He will fill our hearts from His own store,
Giving for every day enough and more.
Beloved, let us love!

EXPERIENCE

Not I, But Christ

. . . We may . . . not be ashamed before Him. . .
1 *John* 2:28

NOT what I am, but what my Saviour is,
Sets my lips free to sing His praises:
Not what I am, but what He is to me,
Makes me cry out to all, 'Oh, taste and see!'

Not what I have, but riches found in Him,
Turn worldly treasure poor and dim:
Not what I have, but what my Lord bestows,
Gives me the courage to oppose His foes.

Not what I say, Christ's Word the Living Bread,
By which the hungry heart is fed:
Not what I say; His Spirit's still small voice
Convicts of sin, bids pardoned souls rejoice.

Not in my strength, but by His Holy Spirit,
I live the Lord's 'Well done' to merit:
Not in my strength, but by my Saviour's grace,
I'll stand at last unshamed before His face.

Talking To Myself

WORSHIP! Worship! Worship! O my soul,
With thy being's whole
Extol the King of glory,
At Whose Word creation's story
Flashed to living fact,
Became God's mighty act!
All created things stood forth
That He might appraise their worth,
Judge them good and set them free,
Each within exact decree,
To perform His will.
Only man, for good or ill,
God made free to choose,
Free to keep or lose,
Gave him love and law,
Reverence to temper awe;
Gave sight, hearing, speech and reason,
All the universe to seize on,
Beauty, music, and a part
In Godlike creative art;
Germ of justice in the mind
God bestowed on all mankind;
Consciousness of life God gave,
Of guilt and of a power to save!
For thy believing
Himself revealing
In Jesus Christ the Lord,
His ever-living Word.
Worship God my soul,
Him Who gives to thy control

Talents having boundless scope
And a heart designed for hope,
Insight to discern the good
That thou mayest hate falsehood.

Worship! Worship! Worship! With thy being's
whole
Praise him! Who breathèd into thee a living soul,
Praise Him! Who made earth fair for thy delight,
Who for thy sake transmuted into love His might,
Who came from Heaven to save thee,
Who all thy sin forgave thee,
Made thee new! Bidding thee walk
In light with Him and freely talk
Of all thy heart's desires;
Learn that His loving kindness never tires,
Who understands thy plight,
Sees far beyond thy sight,
And for thy good in all things
Over-rules for thee and brings
Strength out of weakness, peace in grief,
Enabling thee to trust Him through thy brief
And swiftly passing earthly days.
Now at thy will's command, thy faith can gaze
Through death to see new life prepared,
Eternal joy by loving shared,
Where Jesus is,
And all who love Him are for ever His.
Worship! Worship! Worship! With thy being's
whole,
O my soul!

One Thought Leads To Another

IF I could go back far enough
And peer and pry for long enough,
I might discover how the earth began
And how it was made fit to harbour man.
If I could smash and mend again,
Divide and multiply again,
I'd know the stuff of which the stars are made
And how they hang in space . . . without God's aid.

But all this knowing would not tell
Why I am I! Nor would it tell
What beauty is; nor why my heart turns over
With ecstasy to see the cliffs of Dover,
Lark on wing, sunset on distant seas;
To hear bees in clover, breath of wind in trees,
Or, with attendant sounds, hear Menuhin
Make music playing on a violin!

Sometimes such moments draw me up to Heaven!
Give sense of God, that like a holy leaven
Spreads through my being, waking high resolve,
Making me feel afresh Christ can absolve
Me from past sin and fear, give power new
To know myself God's child, free to pursue
His will, uncloy my mind of thought that chance
A myriad accidents in atom's dance,
Creation void of purpose and of plan,
Could be the origin and end of man.

But knowing God, I now know too
Why I am I! And I know too
That beauty is Divine Love's overspill!

And I'm created with an in-built skill
To joy in it, to feel the thrill of it,
With fresh delight to drink my fill of it
Finding the spring still full! My thirst renewed,
With love of beauty my whole self imbued.

And I am I because God made me so,
The duplicate of none! In embryo
Possessed of every Christlike quality,
Yet vulnerable to all iniquity.
And having only time when I may choose
Which I shall cherish, which decide to lose.
For God imposes liberty
To take my own way. Liberty
To scorn the secret judgments conscience makes,
Reject God's laws and substitute the fakes
That pride or lust or merely love of self
Dictates to bind me, turn my gold to pelf;
Gold God would purify and prove, until
His likeness shone from it, and my own will
In harmony with His, I reach the goal
For which God formed me, made me living soul;
By His grace loving good and loathing ill,
Ready to serve my neighbour, thus fulfil
Christ's rule of love for living; grow to be
Possessed by love, glad in God's company.

And if faith looks on far enough,
And love be loving long enough,
I'll glimpse at times my Heaven and Christ there.
Then, all mysterious here becomes His care;
And while the peace of God rules my heart's core
Christ's gift of joy increases more and more.
As I go marching to my journey's end
Where I shall prove God's doings will transcend
All thoughts of what He has prepared for me,
New beauty, love and life with Him in His eternity.

The Viewpoint

I IN my strength looked down and saw
A very little child – no more;
I in my weakness faltering,
Looked up, and saw that child a King!

I in my joy all eager ran
Unheeding past a burdened man;
I in my sorrow found that He
Lifted me up and carried me!

I in my righteousness passed by
And doubted if God's Christ need die;
I in my guilt crept back to hide
My sin within His wounded side!

A Fool, Poor Love

A FOOL, poor love!
Attempting more than she can do,
Yet if she did not, would she ever know
How far her strength could go?

A fool, poor love!
But it would break her simple heart
To know that of her talents great or small,
She had not given all.

A fool, poor love!
Yet this she well doth understand,
She could not bear to find that of her store
She might have given more!

A fool, poor love!
A happy fool, in paradise,
Giving the loved one all she had to give,
Giving her life, to live!

With Christ I'd Share

. . . Lo, I come to do Thy will, O God. . .
Heb. 10:9

FAILING in gifts, in graces, yet,
With Christ I'd share this likeness still:
I'll cross the threshold of each new-given day
Saying to God, 'I come to do Thy will.'

In The Wood On June 16th*

THERE'S a sound of sighing in the woods today,
As who among the trees should say:
'He does not come for whom the birds are gay,
For whom the flowers stay.'

* Anniversary of my father's death.

There's a sound of sighing in the woods today,
As who among the trees should say:
'We have a lover who has gone away!
Away, away.
We wait, but he is far away.'

To My Mother

DARLING, there is none, here nor there,
Fit to compare
With all the loveliness thou art
To my poor heart.

No one can bestow half the measure,
Half the sweet pleasure,
The peace thy presence brings to me,
Where e'er we be.

Music like thy voice I've not found,
Love's in the sound,
It soothes to sleep my waking fear
And bids hope hear.

There's no lap to rest weary head on
In love's abandon
As is thy lap, where my poor head
May make its bed.

Safely in thy love I may roam
Far, far away from home,
And always find on my returning
Thy love's light burning.

The Return

AFTER long days, I return
To the lone, grey shore!
After long days, fires burn
For me as before.
For me as before, as I had dreamed they would,
Black and gold on the hearth, where all our feet
 have stood.
Close by, green waves still unroll
And the round stones play
Music that wakes in my soul
Past joys and their day.
Past joys and their day, and potent these to call
Happy hopes to the hearth where I may welcome
 all.
No more delays!
After long days
I come
Home!

I return after long days
To the sweet, salt air;
Find all the briar-fringed ways
Surpassingly fair.
Surpassingly fair the ever-changing sea,
White and green at the rim, as was its wont
 to be.
Magic-hued marsh, still serene
Where the sea-birds cry;
Trees on the hill that all lean
Toward the west sky.
Toward the west sky, where fast departing sun

Sometimes leaves his golden robe when fading day is done.
I who did yearn
For these, return,
I come
Home!

After long days I return,
But to love the more;
After long days I discern
Rich beauty's full store;
Rich beauty's full store in fragrant sunlit wood,
Heath and lane and the grass, these each bewitching good;
Health to sad eyes long athirst
For the well-known land;
Balm to a heart that scarce durst
Give hope a free hand.
Give hope a free hand, bid her show me again
Glowing image of home, though it but heighten pain.
From such drear ways,
After long days,
I come
Home!

I return after long days,
And I thank my God
Still I can offer Him praise
For the paths I trod.
For the paths I trod when I felt not His hand
Were the paths God had willed; I went at His command.
He had apportioned my strength,
For each day grace;
Gathered me back home at length,
Oh! well-beloved place.
Oh! well-beloved place where my heart longed to be,

Time and pain are forgot in this blest certainty:
By diverse ways,
After long days,
I've come
Home!

Written on returning to a little house on the Suffolk coast, after long exile through sickness.

God Will Remember

. . . yet will I not forget thee.
Isa. 49:15

'YET will I not forget thee':
This is God's word to me.
He Who spreads out the vasty skies,
He at Whose word the lightning flies,
He in Whose hand creation lies,
He will remember me!

'Yet will I not forget thee':
This is God's word to me.
He Who has called the stars by name,
He Who the devil's might can tame,
He knows my fears, He knows my frame,
He will remember me!

'Yet will I not forget thee':
This is God's word to me.
Though I may falter, faint, and fail,
Though grief and trials make me quail,
Though doubts leap in me and prevail,
He will remember me!

'Yet will I not forget thee':
This is God's word to me.
Here is the righting of all wrong,
Pledge from Him to Whom I belong!
Hope then my heart, my soul be strong,
Thy God remembers thee!

The Lost Song

A FRAGMENT of song came into my head,
A whisper of joy to my heart;
But I was so busy with living and dead,
So closely engaged in life's mart,
That the song slipped away,
And up to this day
I have never again
Heard so sweet a refrain!
But wherever I go,
And whatever I do,
I keep listening and listening
In case some child whistling,
Or bird's song at morn,
Or river's outbourne
Or mother's at eve,
Might help me retrieve
The fragment of song that came into my head;
And if I should catch but a part,
I'd stop all my traffic with living and dead
Until I had learned it by heart.
But perhaps when it fled it stole from my ear
The cunning to know it again,
And I shall go listening to songs far and near,
And always be listening in vain?

War Years

[Jesus said] . . . I am come that they might have life, and that they might have it more abundantly. *John* 10:10

HAND in hand,
Sorrow and death stalk the land,
Blessed are they who do not watch for these,
Nor bow before their tyrannies
But, looking up, beyond, above,
Fix the heart upon God's love;
Draw the heart's desires,
The aspiring flame of all life's fires,
Up to holiness,
Up to the virile loveliness of Godliness;
Use every loss, gain, pain, fall;
Use joys, griefs, trials, triumphs, all
In preparation of the spirit here,
For life's eternal fulness there,
Where enter in no sins,
Where love's abundant life begins,
And God in every heart's felicity
In fair new Salem's City.

Circumstances Alter Cases

I HEARD the yellowhammer
Singing to his love,
And, oh, the sun was shining
And blue the skies above;
And while he went on singing
The sweet bluebells were springing,
But sad my heart with thinking
That my Love was far away;
Sad was my heart with thinking
That my Love was far away.

I heard the bonny robin
Singing to his love,
But then the sun was sinking
And lead the skies above;
And while he went on singing
The cold east wind was whistling,
But glad my heart with thinking
That my Love was home today;
Glad was my heart with thinking
That my Love was home today.

On Listening To The Wireless

LORD, how shall I hear,
When so many voices fill the air far and near?
Speaking in many tongues, speaking in love and
hate,
Cynical sharp clatter, boisterous babel in spate,
Voices insinuating, honeyed, persuasive,
Voices loud-bellowing, raucous, positive,
Cursing, silly-shrill mawkish voices;
Pompous-droning, mulish voices;
Voices complaining, loudly bleating,
Voices mechanical, repeating;
Sound of sinners law defying,
Sound of little children crying.

Lord! Mid all of these, how shall I hear?
And God answers me clear,
'What thou *desirest* to, that thou shalt hear.'

My Little Dog

OH, shall I indulge my fancy
And buy me a little dog?
A dear little lively creature
To set all my mind agog
With a flurry of pleasure and falderal,
Don't you think it would make me a dear little pal?
So, shall I indulge my fancy
And buy me a little dog?

Chorus
YES!

Oh, shall I indulge my fancy
And buy me one of the best?
A bright little Yorkshire terrier
Would never become a pest,
But be funny and frisky and fond of me
And like to be with me wherever I be.
So shall I indulge my fancy
And buy me one of the best?

Chorus
YES!

I am glad I indulged my fancy
And bought me a little pet,
Though she cost me a mint of money
It's a thing I shall not regret,
For she's funny and frisky and fond of me
And likes to be with me wherever I be.
So I'm glad I indulged my fancy
And bought me this dear little pet!

The Wonder

Ye have not chosen Me, but I have chosen you. . .
John 15:16

LOVE went forth one day,
More fair than dawn was He,
But of all who followed in His train
Oh! Wonder! Love chose me!

Wonder greater still,
Love *knows* me now, and yet
A hundred times a day He shows
His love on me is set.

A Doubter's Wish

I WOULD that I could draw near to Christ
As Thomas did that night;
Just to hear Him speak would have sufficed
To turn my dark to light;
To have heard Him say with tenderness,
'Reach hither thou thine hand,'
Would have changed my doubter's wilderness
Into the promised land!
I would,
Oh, I would that I could!

I would that I could have raised my eyes
To meet the love in His,
When He saw poor Thomas trembling rise
And fall upon his knees,
When Christ smiling said, 'Be not faithless,
Believing be!' Ah, that
Would have turned my coward heart's distress
To a magnificat!
I would,
Oh, I would that I could!

I would that I could, but not for me
To know Christ in the flesh,
Nor to touch His wounds, nor yet to see
His miracles afresh,
Nor to walk on the waves, as Peter did,
Nor lean on His breast with John,
Nor to hear Him speak of Heaven and bid
Their troubled hearts trust on.
I would,
Oh! I would that I could!

But what if I could be even as they?
And though I cannot see,
I should yet believe in Christ and say,
'My Saviour, Thou art He,
My Lord and my God!' And trusting turn
My feet into His train?
Would save me from all the hells that burn
And make me His child again.
And I could,
Oh, I could! *If I would!*

Public Behaviour

OH, heart's anguish never need be known;
Never need be known
Save to God alone
That the heart's not turned to stone,
If you smile and smile,
Keep smiling all the while.
But when solitude and night come down
Gone the need for smiling;
Christ will not pass by,
He'll draw nigh;
He, Who knows the heart's not turned to stone
He can set the heart at rest, and He alone.

A Testimony

AS gentle rain to thirsty mead,
So Jesus is to me;
As strength to him who wills a deed,
So Jesus is to me.

As guiding star to mariner,
So Jesus is to me;
As pardon sweet to those who err,
So Jesus is to me.

As peace to those encamped by fear,
So Jesus is to me;
As hope when death has paused too near,
So Jesus is to me.

He Walks With Me

. . . lo, I am with you alway. . . *Matt*. 28:20

HE walked with me
When I was wayward, strong, and proud,
When I denied Him, boasting loud
I knew Him not, nor wished to know
The Man Who said He loved me so.
I doubted whether He could be
My God, yet be so like to me.

In wisdom's husk I clothed me well
And found that Calvary, Heaven and hell
Belonged to days I had outgrown.
I banished them, and chose my own
Ideals of life; and coldly let
Him be unloved, forgot, and yet
He walked with me!

He walked with me!
And when the way grew rough and steep,
And when I called from deep to deep
Of anguish and despair for light
To guide me through my sorrow's night
(For fear and shame and death and sin,
Ah! All of these had entered in
To rob my life of hope and peace)
He said to me, 'It is for this
I walk with thee.'

'I walk with thee
To save, to comfort, and to guide,'
He said, continuing at my side.
But I, though sunk in grief, still sought
For help apart from Him. I thought,
'Could I but find a friend, a man
Akin to me, to whom I can
Unfold the anguish of my heart
And he mayhap can soothe the dart
Of conscience, of remorse, and give
Me comfort that I yet may live.'
I found him not! And in the gloom
Of solitude I thought the doom
Of hell I had denied most fit
(For those forsook by hope taste it
Before 'tis due); and all the way
I travelled thus, by night and day,
He walked with me!

He walked with me,
While I in blinding sorrow cried,
'Oh for a God who would divide
His strength with me and make me new!
That I might live again, and do
Some nobler thing!' Bitter the thought!
Would God stoop down to me who brought
No gift, no praise, but only need,
Deep hungry need? Small hope indeed!
'Twould cost a Calvary to make
A way to me for God! To break
In me the arm of sin, forgive
And set me free, with strength to live
My life aright. If this were done,
'Twould need a Saviour! Is there one?

Oh, blind the eye that would not see
The Son of Man who walked with me!
Oh, deaf the ear that would not hear
The Son of God, His voice so clear!

Strength fled me, knowledge failed, when I
In fear, in shame, with blinded eye,
Stretched forth my hand and longing turned
Toward Him Whom my heart had spurned.
He looked on me; and then I knew
That all I needed He could do;
Knew I had found the friend I sought,
Knew that my pardon had been bought,
Knew that my God was near, not far,
Knew that for me a Saviour, ah!
A Calvary, was found!

Knew One,
The True, the Beautiful, God's Son
Who walks with me!

The Garden

. . . I have called thee by thy name; thou art mine.
Isa. 43:1

OH, I found me in a garden
And I wept!
For while I slept
Came a thief and stole
Innocence
From life's golden bowl.
Left a snake there instead
Rearing its envenomed head,
And I read
In its eye
I must die!

Oh, I found me in a garden
Where they said,
'Christ is dead!'
Wild despair was there,
Hope had fled,
Left the garden bare.
From my heart darkening fear
Spread its terror far and near.
Everywhere
Death and sin
Seemed to win!

Oh, I found me in a garden;
There One came
Who knew my name.
'Lord,' I cried, ''tis Thou!'
Then He smiled,
Stooped to kiss my brow!
And the sweet of His breath
Took away the fear of death;
Fled away the thought of death
When He said,
'Thou shalt live,
I forgive!'

Shall I?

AND shall my heart fear
While Jesus is near?
Though dark be my way
With Him it is day.

And shall He not guide
My feet, at His side,
From crooked to straight
And through Heaven's gate?

There shall I not see
Christ's goodness to me?
And then be content
With all He has sent?

And shall I not now
Stop asking Him how,
Start trusting instead
And thus banish dread?

Two Fools

The fool hath said in his heart, There is no God. . . *Ps.* 14:1

'MY friend,' said he,
'I have decided that there is no God!
And those who think there is, are duped and plod
Through life beclouded, mazed, the slaves of mere
Imagination! Let me now make it clear:
First, much I pondered; then I prayed a prayer;
"O God," I said, "if Thou art anywhere,
Then grant me what I crave, and let the boon
Be mine before the sun shall reach to noon!"
I waited, watched the shadows shrink, and found,
As I had feared to find, there is no ground
For faith in any God! The noontide passed,
My prayer remained unanswered, and the last
Doubt died in me. 'Twas clear God could not be,
Else had He answered, given some sign to me.
So I am free!'

Then spake his friend:
'I too have nursed this matter in my mind;
Have cogitated much thereon and find
That my conclusion matches thine, though I
Have only now perceived the reason why
I do agree with thee. I also prayed;
I asked that rain might fall. I was afraid
The dust would spoil the freshness of my grass.
Straightway the clouds appeared. It rained!
Alas!
For I remembered then my wife had planned

That day to entertain her mother, and
The feast was spread beneath the garden trees
Where rain would mar the whole affair and these,
Her schemes, fail of intent, which was to gain
Help from the lady (she is rich) to train
Our son as an astrologer. "Oh stop
The rain, great God!" I cried. The final drop
Fell as I spoke. This must have been mere chance,
For no true God would deign to serve and dance
Attendance on man's passing plans, I know.
Therefore I gave up God for good, and so
Faith had an end!'

Thus spake two fools!
To which of them am I akin that I
Should ground my faith in God and all His high
And holy purposes, on this poor test
Of whether He or I shall know the best,
Most Godlike answer to a prayer of mine?
Faith must strike root more deeply far, combine
The prayer of strong desire with a true
And full submission to God's will; and through
His word or through His silences, discern
What He would say to me His child; and learn
To wait with patience and to run with zeal.
Yea, this and more must faith do; set the seal
Of works to her beliefs, and lead me so
To love my God, as well as trust; for though
'Tis faith reveals God, 'tis by love we come
To know Him and to trust, nor change, as some,
Their faith to fit prevailing whim; for they
Who love God seek no sign but to obey
And honour Him.

This will I do, and still
Believing, follow Him, rest in His will,
And dare to know God is.

Grace Enough For Me

. . . My grace is sufficient for thee. . .
2 *Cor.* 12:9

WHEN my heart was dark and sinful,
Hungry for the living Bread,
Jesus brought me full Salvation
By the Blood He shed;
And whilst walking in His favour,
From my sins and doubts set free,
There is grace enough in Jesus,
Grace enough for me!

When the clouds of sorrow darken
All my sky and hide God's face,
And my heart is faint with seeking
Love it cannot trace;
When my soul is tossed and toiling
On temptation's stormy sea,
There is grace enough in Jesus,
Grace enough for me!

Though my future lies all hidden,
Yet the heart of God doth know
All the way He hath appointed
That my soul shall go;
And I trust in His sure promise,
Whatso'er my lot may be,
There'll be grace enough in Jesus,
Grace enough for me!

Written to be sung to the tune On the Banks of Allen Water.

Resolved

I'LL walk no more in ways of my own choosing,
No more return to pleasures born of sin;
My heart is fixed, for Christ this life I'm losing
That I with Him eternal life may enter in.

I'll work no more for wealth of this world's making,
No more search out a treasure that decays;
I look to Christ, and all for Him forsaking
I dedicate my days to my Redeemer's praise.

I'll doubt no more the love and power of Jesus,
No more forget His mercy to my soul;
Life, Truth and Way, oh He to me is precious!
I'll trust and serve and love Him with my being's
whole.

I Will

COME my soul make answer,
Jesus waits to hear,
Wilt thou leave thy sinning?
Wilt thou leave thy fear?
Jesus waits to pardon,
Jesus waits to save,
Come my soul make answer,
Wilt thou seek Him now?

I will seek my Saviour,
Seek my Saviour now.

Come my soul make answer,
Jesus waits for thee,
Calls thee swift to follow,
Calls thee sin to flee;
Jesus waits to lead thee
Upward to thy God,
Come my soul make answer,
Wilt thou follow now?

I will follow Jesus,
Follow Jesus now.

Come my soul make answer,
Jesus waits to know,
Wilt thou trust Him fully,
Bid thy doubting go?
Jesus waits to fill thee
With abounding power,
Come my soul make answer,
Wilt thou trust Him now?

I will trust my Saviour,
Trust my Saviour now.

Come my soul make answer,
Jesus shows His hands
Wounded for thy healing,
Speaks His love's demands;
Asks thee for thy service,
Willing, constant, true;
Come my soul make answer,
Wilt thou serve Him now?

I will serve my Saviour,
I will serve Him now.

Written to be sung.

Singing To Myself In Youth

UP my soul, take heart of grace,
Christ the Lord is in this place
Where the humble-hearted bow,
Christ is here to help thee now.

Up my soul, attempt, achieve;
They who on their Lord believe
Need not lean on human power,
Nor await propitious hour.

Up my soul, the challenge sounds,
Up, and go where sin abounds;
Answer Christ Who calls for thee,
'Here am I, my Lord, send me.'

The Garment

And he, casting away his garment, rose, and came to Jesus. *Mark* 10:50

CAST away thy pride, my soul,
Cast away thy pride!
Very humble thou must be,
If Christ's glory thou would'st see,
Glory of His littleness,
Human birth and helplessness.
Pride of place and pride of mind,
These, my soul, will never find

That so lowly manger bed
Where He laid His kingly head.
Would'st thou enter where He is,
See the beauty that is His?
Cast away thy pride, my soul,
Cast away thy pride!

Cast away thy doubt, my soul,
Cast away thy doubt!
Strong in faith thy heart must be,
If Christ's triumph thou would'st see;
On the lonely mountain side,
Or in surging human tide,
See His pure divinity,
See His meek humanity
Triumph over fiends and fears,
Human suffering and tears.
Would'st thou get thee eyes that can
See Him God, and know Him man?
Cast away thy doubt, my soul,
Cast away thy doubt!

Cast away thy fear, my soul,
Cast away thy fear!
If Christ's dying thou would'st see,
Love must reign in thee, for he
Whom love rules hath cast out fear!
Then to Calvary draw near;
Dare to look on Him; behold,
In His eyes, the love men sold
Unto death.
But from the grave
He brought victory – should save
All men from death's sting. Would'st taste
Such sweet liberty? Oh, haste!
Cast away thy fear, my soul,
Cast away thy fear!

Cast away thy sin, my soul,
Cast away thy sin!
If Christ's life thy heart would share,
Sin must not be lurking there.
Would'st thou know that Jesus lives?
Prove how freely He forgives?
For when He has given peace,
Then thy heart shall know He is
Now alive to intercede
For all sinners in their need.
Would'st thou in Christ's life have part
And be gathered to His heart?
Cast away thy sin, my soul,
Cast away thy sin!

Two Views Of Man

I

THINK of man's little heart, and pity him!
Who must attempt so great a thing as life,
Be found a living part of the stern strife
'Twixt good and evil raging from the dim
Half-hidden past to this his present day.
Great powers within his reach pursue their course,
Whilst he, though oft uncertain of the source
His own thoughts spring from, is content to pray
A passing peace or pleasure, and to seek
Pathways of ease nor heed where they may lead;
His cup as shallow as his thirst is weak,
A drop doth him suffice though his full mead
Stands waiting. Strangest of mysteries:
Man doth not yet aspire to what is his!

II

Think on his soaring heart, and pity man!
Who must imprison so strong desire within
The narrow bounds of his weak flesh, begin,
From babyhood, to match supine 'I can'
With vigorous 'I would'. Oh, vain essay!
For while his strength is meted out in short
Uncertain spells, the heart of him is caught
By myriad unexplored desires; the way
Called knowledge stretches far beyond his sight.
Eager he treads it, yet he cannot fill
His thirst for truth, his longing for the height,
Which, ever distant, charms and draws him still.
Oh hungry soul of man, how strange that God
Ties such a spirit to an earthly clod!

Delusion

Chance alone is at the source . . . of all creation . . . pure chance.
Monod

Our world is like a convoy lost in darkness on an unknown coast . . . the world of our everyday reality is no more than a more or less entertaining or distressful story thrown upon a cinema screen. The story holds together . . . But the sceptical mind says stoutly, 'This is delusion.'
H. G. Wells

COME then, deluded be with me!
If *this* delusion be,
That in everything I see
Witness to a Master mind,
Token that the Lord is kind.
Crystal, star, the universe,
Or pompous beetle moving in reverse,
Each one to its uses so exactly suited,
Each to its Maker's taste embeautied,
Speak to me of law and plan,
Of God's relationship to man;
Even flowers of grass,
Swiftly as they pass,
Show such delicate design
That one searching for a sign,
In the grass would have it;
There might start the happy habit
Of relating all to God;
And one could on any sod
Find the same authority
For Divine ubiquity.

But if *this* be madness,
Life's condemned to sadness!
Farthest Pisgah sight
Can't postpone the night:
Beauty is less real than I,
End of mankind's but to die;
There's no speech, only a cry,
A cry and no reply;
Homing instinct in the soul,
But no home, no goal!
And time, a treacherous sea spread wide
In failing light, with racing tide
Where life's without an ark,
Sinking in the dark . . .

But is not *this* stark madness?
Madness without gladness!
Come, then, deluded be with me,
For in everything I see
Witness to a Master mind,
Token that the Lord is kind,
Token that by His intent
Man for holiness is meant,
Meant for lasting love and joy,
Joy without alloy.

This is no delusion
But rescue from confusion,
Restoring to its pristine beauty
Life in time and in eternity;
For life abundant Jesus gives,
One who trusts Him by Him lives
And finds a new delight in living,
Has new expectancies, believing
All God's promises, walks on rejoicing, trusting,
Has light in darkness, peace in war, by faith still
  thrusting
Ever farther into the unknown;
Begins to see more clearly that God is on the throne,

That life and matter,
Their every trace and tatter,
Their intricate and beautiful designs,
Stem from a living mind; that man himself holds
signs
Of the Creator's care, God's love the lifespring,
The origin and energy of everything.
Is this delusion?
No! Logical conclusion;
For every seeking soul the dawn of truth
Dispelling dark of man's mere guessing as
uncouth.
Grotesque the idea that man and all existences
With all their ordered harmonies
Are accidental combinations without meaning,
The so-called laws of nature spawned of mindless
seeming,
And man, the masterpiece,
By these mean fallacies
Robbed of his right to choose the good,
Rejects the concept of God's Fatherhood,
Himself a living soul, God's child;
Concocts his own drear version of the cosmos, is
beguiled
Into the catastrophic folly of concluding
Chance the cause of all that is, which leaves him
still eluding
The ever-present question: for what purpose his
creation?
Leaves unexplained his moments of elation,
And equally ignores his long and comfortless
despairs,
While scientists and artists, splitting hairs
On problems far removed from daily living,
Pile doom on doom, till life itself seems not worth
having.
And youngsters in their teens, ignoring all life's
joys,

Die by their own hands! Their lovely bodies left like
broken toys
Upon time's refuse heap.
Dear children, choosing at life's dawn, death's
night, thus reap
The harvest of their unbelief,
For all who love them multiplying grief!
But this must be illusion,
Death-dealing dark delusion.
For still the heavens declare the glory of God, and
still
Earth clothed in beauty wakens man's delight, and
still
Thought and love move heart of all mankind.
Still, he who looks may see God in Christ's face and
find
New life and rest unto his soul;
Find love to God and man,
The joyous ecstasy of life wove through the whole;
Receive a vision of God's will, man's highest good,
And God man's friend.
On this builds life, trusting His God
Who says 'Lo! I am with you to the end.'

And this is not delusion
But heavenly infusion,
Light on our way,
Strength for today.
Oh come, rejoice with me,
For in everything I see
Witness to a Master mind,
Token that the Lord is kind!

Memory And I In Suffolk

MEMORY called for me the other day
And we set off together,
I lent my feet to memory's sway
And we went walking far away,
Far, far away from now.

Flow'rs were blooming there I'd seen before,
When we were there together,
And breathed the air along that shore
Where seas are sighing ever more,
Far, far away from now.

Larks on rapid wing were rising high
And singing altogether,
Their music seemed to fill the sky
As when we heard them, you and I,
Far, far away from now.

Suddenly my heart felt light and free
From time and death together,
I saw God make all good agree
In one harmonious ecstasy,
Not far away from now.

Desire

I WANT to live in the flat lands
Where I can see the sky,
Where I can look to wide horizons
As I watch the evening die;
Where I can see the north grow rosy
As midsummer night draws nigh;
Oh, let me live in the flat lands
Where I can see the sky!

I want to live in the flat lands
Where shadows do not stay,
Where sun makes pause upon the earth's rim
At dawn ev'ry cloudless day
To take in glorious effulgence
Around Heaven's arch its way;
Oh, let me live in the flat lands
Where shadows do not stay!

I want to live in the flat lands
Where roads run straight and far,
Where great elms stand all stiff and stately
And where quiet waters are
Where, sometimes, I can see reflected
Both the new moon and her star;
Oh, let me live in the flat lands
Where roads run straight and far!

I want to live in the flat lands,
Breathe ev'ry air that blows,
See the windmill's arms upclimbing
With a sense of calm repose;
Low or high, singing or double,
Have sight of all rainbows;
Oh, let me live in the flat lands,
Breathe ev'ry wind that blows!

I want to live in the flat lands
Where larks sing day and night!
Where linnets perch on the golden gorse
Pouring out their heart's delight;
Where I can hear in spring and autumn
The wild geese pass on their flight;
Oh, let me live in the flat lands
Where larks sing day and night!

I want to live in the flat lands
Where I can see the skies,
Where, from a house with many windows
On the brow of a gentle rise,
I may look out in any weather
And let skies content my eyes;
Oh, let me live in the flat lands
Where I can see the skies!

The Open Door

God that made the world. . . Lord of heaven and earth . . . in Him we live, and move, and have our being. . . *Acts* 17:24, 28

MY soul! Hope thou in God! How else go on?
How look on life if hope in God be gone?
How bear the loneliness of all creation
If God be absent from thy contemplation?
How know thyself and what thou might'st yet be,
Could'st thou not look on Christ in hope to see?
My soul! Hope thou in God and fuller prove
Thou hast thy being in Him, dost live and move
Because God is, Who doth and will sustain
All that He makes, and will thy life maintain,
Whom He commands to stand upright before Him,
Giving thee will to trust, and instinct to adore Him.
Hope thou in God, go on to hope, hope still,
Be His face hidden and obscured His will,
Though He be silent to thee, hope on, for
Thy hope in Him shall be an open door
Through which thy God Himself shall pass to bless
And show thee secretly His loveliness.
Thus, O my soul, when other hopes of thine decline
  and fail,
Hope in thy God, His love and power shall flourish
  and prevail.

Retrospect And Prospect

IN temptation I am not alone,
In serving sinners not left solitary,
In haste to deal with things undone
Can ever count on Christ to strengthen me.
And so when now He makes me down to lie
In pastures green by pleasant waters resting,
I will not doubt His love will lead
And keep me safe in every future testing.

Fear not, dear heart,
The Shepherd's part
Christ will in faithfulness fulfil,
And now, in life or death, thee keep and comfort
still.

A Divided Heart

. . . Thou shalt love the Lord thy God with all thy heart. . .
Luke 10:27

OH, swift is Joy to part
From a divided heart.

As swift clouds over-run
And hide the shining sun,
So swift are Doubts to spread
Their gloom where Joy did tread.
And swift to flee their shade
Springs forth young Faith, afraid;
For swift is Fear to heel
Of Doubt, as dust to wheel.
Then swift of foot and still
Flies Peace from bold Self-will,
Who swift struck down and tied
Sweet Love's fair hands and cried,
'Be swift, Pride! Bar the door,
Here let us have no more
That swift heart medicine
Called penitence for sin.'
So swift calamity
O'ertakes lost unity!

Oh, swift is Joy to part
From a divided heart.

Be Glad For Me!

. . . all forsook Him, and fled. *Mark* 14:50

OH, pity all mankind, that none was found
Faithful and proudly glad to stand his ground
At Jesu's side
When Jesus died!

Oh, pity! No one dared cry out and shout
Defiance at the tyrants who put out
The light in Jesu's eyes
And left the dark of lies
To be man's guide
When Jesus died!

Oh, pity all mankind, that of all those
Whom Jesus loved and blessed, not one arose
To plead in His defence
His lovely innocence,
Or show a straightened limb
Or sight restored by Him.
In proof of good He'd done,
Of all Christ healed, not one
To rush among the hostile crowd
Trembling, gesticulating,
Shouting, expostulating,
Telling how dead were raised,
Blind giv'n sight, and joy-mazed
Lame made leap!
Not one, for Love to weep
And cry 'Slay me instead,
But do not will Christ dead,

Who at our call
Would save us all!'
Alas! Not one thus crying,
And Jesus near to dying. . .

Oh, pity all mankind!
(Proud dust, hard heart, blind mind!)
To rescue Him
Or die with Him
None tried
When Jesus died!

. . . Christ . . . Who loved me, and gave Himself for me.
Gal. 2:20

But pity *me* of all mankind that I,
For whom Christ Jesus came to die,
His Godhead now revealed,
By His up-rising sealed,
By Holy Ghost attested,
By my own heart invested
With kingly rights in me –
Oh, pity me,
That I can doubt Him,
And let my fears drive me to flout Him!

Oh, pity me! So swift to judge mankind,
Who now worse guilt in my own mind must find;
That knowing Him and loving,
Praising, adoring,
I, who in secret, joy my Lord to name Him,
Yet before men by silences can shame Him!
Now, when Christ Jesus lives,
And I share life He gives,
Add this, as though past sin had not sufficed,
That I, whom He forgave, am yet sometimes
ashamed of Christ!

But none will pity me, oh no!
One only reads my heart and knows my woe,
That One Who bled for me,
He cares
How my soul fares;
He grieves to see me fail,
But does not rail.
Oh, I must weep, yes weep and laugh to know it,
He owns His love, and will on me bestow it!
Unmatched the mystery
Christ looks on me with pity!
And in pure shining of His eyes
Withers self-love and dies.

Be glad for me,
There's Love for me!
And by Love's life, I will so live, so love, so die,
That men shall testify
When I have died,
'*She* was on Jesu's side!'

ON DEATH AND ETERNITY

Life's Road

LOVE came down this road
T'ward penury and pain,
Love came down this road
Nor turned Him back again.

Love came all alone
To suffer and be slain,
Slighted by His own,
Yet turned not back again.

Love searched all this ground
To find the souls of men,
I had not been found
Had He turned back again.

If Love had turned back
Before I let Him die,
Life had been but wrack
And I no power to fly.

Love came down this road
And trod it to the end,
Went t'wards Jerusalem,
There made death my friend.

Died, and broke death's bands,
Destroyed the power of sin,
Opened with His wounded hands
Heaven's gate to let me in.

I now walk this road,
But safely I shall go
On to Love's abode,
For Love the way will show.

Now I Know

AH! I was in the hills of Heaven*
Just while an angel counted seven;
A living breath filled all my being;
Content at last the eye with seeing.
The heart in ecstasy safe held
Forgot all fear, and joy unquelled
Set all the mind alight with beauty,
Made even of hard-featured duty
A thing all reasonable and sweet
That I was fit and glad to meet.
All was at peace, all solved, all known
That needed knowing, when alone,
High folded in that secret place,
Soul slipped the bounds of time and space,
And silent, felt eternity
A near familiar verity;
Believed the truth, so far above me,
God made me for Himself to love me;
Knew of His love God gives what is,
Knew of His love that I am His!

Yes! I was in the hills of Heaven
Just while an angel counted seven.
And now I know,
However far across the dusty plains I go,
However long my days down here may be,
That I have breathed Heaven's airs and they
agree with me.

* Gratefully acknowledging the first line of Mary Webb's exquisite poem, 'The Hills of Heaven'.

Harbinger

THE echo of eternity is brought
By love into man's narrow heart; the sense
Of long or short in time is changed for tense
Unmeasurable anguish at the thought
Love may be lost; or, instantly, is brought
Back to the present where love lives, and whence
The lover never would remove. From thence
The past seems shrunken to a flash; and fraught
With every joy, a living love doth seem
To testify it must for ever be
What now is. Of end, love cannot dream;
But in the future steadfastly doth see
The promise of increased intensity,
A harbinger of immortality.

My Calvary

'PREPARE thee for thy Calvary,'
Whispered a still small voice to me.
And soughing breeze
And sighing seas
Seemed to repeat, 'Prepare!
Prepare!'
And often if my heart were gay,
If joy and beauty filled a day,

The shadow of that thought would creep
Across my soul, or mar my sleep.
I cried to God and prayed that He
Would fit me for my Calvary,
That troubled morn
When day would dawn
Which held for me
My Calvary.

It came;
The cross, the cries, the pain, the shame;
But 'twas not I
Whom they led forth to die:
It was the one I loved!

Love Keeps Silence

TIME and death together say,
'Love must fail.
Life is but a passing day,
We prevail.'

Death and time together say,
'We have won!
Love will never find a way
To love on!'

Love keeps silence, smiles and waits,
Seems to know
Time and death are but the gates
Through which she'll go.

Time Moves

TIME swiftly moves to close the door we pass,
In silence closes what now shall no more open:
And he who negligently passes by
The call of duty, or love's gentler prompting,
Shall find himself at close of day pursued
By whispering phantoms time can never banish,
The might-have-beens which now can never be . . .

Eternal Things

. . . the things which are not seen are eternal.
2 *Cor*. 4:18

ON! To our journey's end!
Christ still our Friend;
And still, our joy
In His employ
To work His will.
And trusting still,
Live for eternal things,
Till death shall give us wings!

He Hath Set Eternity In Their Hearts

HERE we prepare for Heaven.
By time's swift flight
Become aware that even
Longest life's too slight,
Too short, too incomplete,
Too palpably unfinished part
To give love what is meet
To satisfy the heart
Where God Himself has set for thee
Eternity.

Content?

CONTENT with Time? How can I be?
My heart holds love's as yet unfathomed spring,
My mind is all agog with questioning,
How could time be enough for me?

Time comes in fragments swiftly past,
The moments I would keep dissolve like smoke,
The threads of joy love wove through life, Time
broke,
And time itself will end at last.

Time's not enough for simple ploys
Like seeing bluebells blooming in the spring,
Like walking in the low hills while larks sing.
Time soon runs out for such sweet joys.

Time's always short when I am glad!
As when with those I love we talk and laugh.
To play with children Time's too short by half!
Too short for grief when I am sad.

Content with Time? No I am not!
I have so many things to thank God for,
Such longing to love Him, and others, more;
I can't if Time be all I've got!

If *Time* be all I have to spend,
Why should my heart aspire to things so high?
Love, born eternal, be condemned to die?
I, be created but to *end*?

Time does not fit with what I am!
Silence and memory kindle in me thought
Needing new speech! To learn it Time's too short
And soon becomes a kind of sham.

Content with Time? Not any more!
For I have looked upon eternity,
Heard voice of truth in pure simplicity!
Far beyond Time my thoughts now soar.

Treasure

. . . treasures in Heaven . . . for where your treasure is, there will your heart be also. *Matt.* 6:20, 21

TOO late! Too late!
No time for any new debate.
Too late to spread before my eyes
Riches within my grasp: I *have* a prize!
All meanly gotten wealth's forsworn,
All worldly wisdom looks outworn
In glow of what I know!
My heart's been told, and so
I'm on my way to reach the skies,
For there my treasure lies.

Musing

HOW strange that I shall soon be dead
Who feel so full of life,
Whose thoughts spring ceaseless in my head,
Whose heart with hope is rife;
Who know so many questions, need
But time to find reply,
But time to taste fruit from the seed
I set. But I must die!
Yet is death's very incongruity
Sign I was made for immortality.

Thoughts On How Death May Come

AT Thy word I'll lie me down,
I'll lie me down to die.
At Thy word I'll lie me down, say goodbye,
Say goodbye to all the loveliness of earth and sky.

At Thy word I will lay down,
Lay down my hands to rest.
At Thy word I'll fold my hands on my breast,
Fold my hands, to work no more at anyone's behest.

At Thy word I'll seal my lips,
My voice shall silent be,
Silent, though I long to speak tenderly,
Tenderly to those I love and tell Thy love to me.

At Thy word I'll close my eyes,
My eyes shall look no more,
Look no more on anything seen before.
Look no more on face of those I love this side death's door.

At Thy word I'll lie me down,
I'll lie me down to wait,
Wait until Thou bid me come through Heaven's gate,
Through Heaven's gate to breathe new life and take my new estate.

Secret Thoughts Of A Believer On Death's Doorstep

OLD, worn, ugly; feeble smile hovering
about lips, eyes closed.

I see a place where hopes come true,
A place where I shall be with Christ, and you,
A place of perfect bliss
Where I shall *know* that 'Heaven *is* this!'

Jesus Lives

JESUS lives! And therefore I
Need not fear to live or die.

Jesus lives! So I may rest
My sick soul upon His breast.

Jesus lives! So I may face
Every trial by His grace.

Jesus lives! So I may plead
At God's throne in time of need.

Jesus lives! So I may go
Strong to succour lost and low.

Jesus lives! So I may dwell
Safely on the brink of hell.

Jesus lives! And therefore I
Do not fear to live or die!

The Saviour All-Sufficient

JESUS Christ, to me
Is, and still will be:
In darkness light,
In weakness might,
In trial grace,
In sorrow solace,
In tempest rest,
In doubt behest,
In joy my peace,
In bonds release,
In life my glory,
In death victory!

Index of first lines

A

A fitful silence steals upon the wood 93
A fool, poor love 158
A fragment of song came into my head 164
A robin sang one morning 97
A soldier of the King of kings 81
After long days, I return 161
Ah! I was in the hills of Heaven 202
And oh, the gold of autumn, the emerald of spring 91
And shall my heart fear 175
Art thou poor, forlorn, and lost 119
As gentle rain to thirsty mead 171
At one with my Lord 80
At thy word I'll lie me down 209

B

Beloved, let us love 149
Beloved, the birds are all singing in March 98

C

Cast away thy pride, my soul 181
Come and praise the Lord with me 11
Come, blessed Jesus, come 51
Come, dear one, look on these 102
Come my soul make answer 179
Come then, deluded be with me 185
Come with Thy rod, O Lord, and make my languid zeal 45
Content with Time? How can I be 206

D
Darling Grandma hear us sing 123
Darling, there is none, here nor there 160
December 110
Dull, dismal, desolate days 134

F
Failing in gifts, in graces, yet 159
For friend what shall I pray 55

G
Go your ways 29
Grief is ever old 124

H
Hand in hand 165
Has hope anything to say 134
He speaks in language I can understand 19
He walked with me 171
Here are prepared the instruments of Love 27
Here comes fresh February 99
Here we prepare for Heaven 206
Holy Spirit, work in me 54
Hope lies dying 132
Hope of the world! Through all its sorrow 37
How blest it were to seek the lost with Thee 79
How frigidly, how frigidly 94
How long would it take to thank God for the rose 113
How strange that I shall soon be dead 208
How would mankind rejoice 35
Hunger and the cold 74

I
I heard the yellow-hammer 166
I in my strength looked down and saw 158

I know a summer garden 115

I love the sound of my Saviour's voice 133
I love the wide grey stretches of the skies 128
I saw pure beauty animate in light 104
I see Thee, Lord, a little child upon Thy knee 42
I used to think the singing of the birds in spring 131
I want to live in the flat lands 190
I was walking alone among the trees 99
I would that I could draw near to Christ 169
If I could go back far enough 156
If my heart should falter in a time of stress 48
I'll walk no more in ways of my own choosing 179
In November bitter sweet 106
In temptation I am not alone 193
In the valley, on the hill 96

J
Jesus Christ the sinner's Saviour 84
Jesus Christ, to me 211
Jesus lives! And therefore I 210
Jesus, oh let there be on me 49

K
King Thou art of my heart 65

L
Let not hope disturb thee, no! Nor let thine eyes 36
Let us together thank God for today 64
Like the music of the water flowing ever through the wood 125
Little Jinks was up to larks 75
Look on my heart Lord, read the word unspoken 52
Look to the past's long night 16
Lord, how shall I hear 167
Lord, let me in to where Thou art at last 61
Lord! Let me walk 58
Lord let Thy tenderness 53
Love came down this road 201

LOVE said to love, 'Come and see!' 147
Love went forth one day 168
Lower than angels Jesus came 22

M
Memory called for me the other day 189
'My friend,' said he 176
My soul! Hope thou in God! How else go on 192

N
Never man spake like this Man 38
No sound discordant, none too low to lend 93
Not as mighty river 59
Not to destroy, but to save 25
Not what I am, but what my Saviour is 153

O
O Christ! Would I had ever been all clean 49
O Lord, give time for earthly knowing 60
O Lord! How great a joy had I some gift 67
O Lord, how happy I could be 66
O Lord of life Whose Name is Love 60
O loving Lord 43
O Prince of Peace, who shall Thy subjects be 28
O willing feet of Jesus 41
Oh, beauty! Oh, grace 92
Oh! Ev'ry land is filled with sin 73
Oh, for the strength of ten 85
Oh, God be praised for the holly tree 114
Oh, God be thanked for gentle summer rain 94
Oh, have you seen the Army come marching down our street 71
Oh! Have you seen the gold come in, in October 105
Oh, heart's anguish never need be known 170
Oh, I found me in a garden 174
Oh, I have been so happy 121
Oh, joy 34

Oh, let there be 46
Oh, Love of God most precious 63
Oh, low they laid Him at His birth 23
Oh, meet 112
Oh, pity all mankind, that none was found 195
Oh, sad the day 136
Oh, shall I indulge my fancy 167
Oh! Strange, that from the dim mysterious past 12
Oh, swift is Joy to part 194
Oh! The pain of sorrow 119
Oh! Where shall I weep for my Beloved 130
Old, worn, ugly; feeble smile hovering 210
On! To our journey's end 205

P
Pauper in all but tears 141
Poor Peter thrice denied 142
'Prepare thee for thy Calvary' 203
Prevent me, Lord, from going where I would 50

R
Rest in this, poor heart: God knows 127

S
She did not wait to be invited 121
Silver bells and running water 91
Sometimes it seems that I have never wept 139
Still shines His light, piercing the deepest gloom 37

T
Thank Thee, O Lord, for coming here 65
That men might see God, Jesus clothed Himself in clay 17
That's all ended! What a pity 146
The echo of eternity is brought 203
The hills are clothed with majesty 47

The larks are singing in all this lovely land 126
The purpling buds all swelled with rising sap 101
The silent morning swathed in grey 103
The sound of my dear one's voice to me 129
The west wind is blowing 114
There's a sound of sighing in the woods today 159
They say the fields were all in flower 26
Think of man's little heart, and pity him 183
Thou art the Way 20
Though tossed by temptation 138
Time and death together say 204
Time swiftly moves to close the door we pass 205
To Christ thy King 44
Too late! Too late! 208

U

Up my soul, take heart of grace 181

W

We have loved and we have chosen 86
What are popularity 83
What if my heart be 135
When Jesus came to Bethlehem 18
When my heart was dark and sinful 178
When sickness comes and all my
plans lie shattered 139
When the heart is ready 80
Worship! Worship! Worship! O my soul 154

Y

'Yet will I not forget thee' 163